The Quaker community in Ballymurray

Maynooth Studies in Local History

SERIES EDITOR Michael Potterton

The six volumes in the MSLH series for 2024 cover a broad chronological and geographical canvas across four provinces, focusing variously on people, places, families, communities and events. It begins with an unlikely search for Vikings in the north-west of Ireland, where the evidence is more compelling than most people realize. Further south, in Carrick-on-Shannon, we trace the fortunes of the St George family from the Plantation of Leitrim through to the decades after the Famine. From Carrick we continue south to Ballymurray in Roscommon and its Quaker community (1717–1848), including their relationship with the Croftons of Mote Park. Further south still, in 1701 Jacobite Patrick Hurly of Moughna, Co. Clare, was at the centre of a 'sham robbery' of gold and jewellery worth about €500,000 in today's money. Unlike Hurly, Mary Mercer was renowned for her charitable endeavours, including the establishment of a shelter for orphaned girls in Dublin three hundred years ago in 1724. Finally, the last volume in this year's crop examines the evolution of the resilient farming community at Carbury in Co. Kildare.

* * *

Raymond Gillespie passed away after a very short illness on 8 February 2024. He had established the Maynooth Studies in Local History (MSLH) series with Irish Academic Press in 1995, from which time he served as series editor for a remarkable 27 years and 153 volumes. Taking over those editorial reins in 2021, my trepidation was tempered by the knowledge that Raymond agreed to remain as an advisor. True to his word, he continued to recommend contributors, provide peer-review, mentor first-time authors (and series editors) and give sound advice. Shoes that seemed big to fill in 2021 just got a lot bigger.

Maynooth Studies in Local History: Number 166

The Quaker community in Ballymurray, Co. Roscommon, 1718–1848

Jacqueline née Creaven d'Towey

FOUR COURTS PRESS

Set in 11.5pt on 13.5pt Bembo by
Carrigboy Typesetting Services for
FOUR COURTS PRESS LTD
7 Malpas Street, Dublin 8, Ireland
www.fourcourtspress.ie
and in North America for
FOUR COURTS PRESS
c/o IPG, 814 N Franklin Street, Chicago, IL 60610

© Jacqueline née Creaven d'Towey and Four Courts Press 2024

ISBN 978-1-80151-159-9

All rights reserved. Without limiting the rights under copyright reserved alone, no part of this publication may be reproduced, stored in or introduced into a retrieval system, or transmitted, in any form or by any means (electronic, mechanical, photocopying, recording or otherwise), without the prior written permission of both the copyright owner and the above publisher of this book.

Printed in Ireland
by Sprint Books, Dublin

Contents

Acknowledgments	6
Introduction	7
1 The beginning of the Ballymurray Quaker community, 1716–41	14
2 Ballymurray Quakers and their locality, 1741–88	26
3 The decline of the Ballymurray Quaker community, 1789–1848	41
Conclusion	57
Appendix	59
Notes	60
Abbreviations	60
Index	67

FIGURES

1 Ballymurray Quaker meeting house	7
2 Map of Ballymurray Quaker meeting house and surrounds	9
3 Mote Park house	11

TABLES

1 Twenty Ballymurray Quakers, 1818	43
2 Ballymurray area landholdings, 1827	49

Acknowledgments

This work is based on research conducted for an MA in Local History at the University of Limerick from 2021 to 2022 under course director David Fleming. I would like to offer my sincere thanks to my supervisor, Liam Chambers of Mary Immaculate College, for his never-failing encouragement and patience and his invaluable guidance and assistance with my endeavours to do justice to this study. Thank you. I am thankful to David Fleming and the lecturers who provided the MA in Local History. During the Covid pandemic the delivery of the course remained professional and accessible. I am grateful for the assistance of the many generous librarians of the institutions visited for this research: Glucksman Library, UL; Roscommon County Library, Roscommon; Friends Historical Library, Dublin; National Archives of Ireland; National Library of Ireland. I am very grateful to Roscommon County Council who awarded me the 2022 Heritage research bursary, which allowed me to access many research materials. I am especially grateful to my family who all assisted me in practical IT skills and proof-reading. To Michelle, my solicitor friend who provided explanation of 'notice parties': thank you for your assistance. To the students I journeyed with in our research: your friendship and kindness meant the world to me. To Caitlín Browne and Tricia Pluski Creaven for proof-reading and excellent advice: thank you. To my fellow genealogist and historian Eilish of 'Irishclannconnections': your enthusiasm, encouragement and assistance have been inspirational. My sincere thanks to you all.

Introduction

Ballymurray Quaker meeting house stands just off the N61, three miles (4.8km) south of Roscommon town (fig. 1). Built in 1721, it was the business and worship premises for a small community of Quaker families until 1848, when the local meeting was discontinued.[1] Ballymurray's significance lies in the fact that it was the only Quaker community in Connacht to survive longer than twenty years. Drawing on a wide range of sources, this book presents the first substantial study of the community, charting its origins and development over the course of the eighteenth century, as well as its struggle for survival and eventual demise in the first half of the nineteenth century.

1. Ballymurray Quaker meeting house, April 2023 (image courtesy of Una Sugrue)

The Society of Friends, more commonly known as the Quakers, was founded by George Fox of Leicestershire, England, in 1652. By 1654 the first recorded Friends' meetings in Ireland took place in

Lurgan, Co. Armagh, at the home of William Edmundson.[2] Olive C. Goodbody explains 'the worship of the society has from its beginning been based on a quiet waiting on God, so that his Spirit may be revealed in the heart of each person'.[3] A core belief was that the Spirit could be found equally in each person and therefore the Society did not require paid ministers. In the absence of a priesthood, the Society was managed by meetings of its members: minutes, together with records of births, marriages and deaths, were recorded and preserved with great care.[4] The meetings provided for governance within a tiered system encompassing a local meeting (Ballymurray), a monthly meeting (Moate), a provincial meeting and a national meeting, which took place in Dublin. Ballymurray Quaker community was small; its origins lay with six families who settled in the area from the late 1710s and it was placed under the care of the Moate meeting, approximately twenty-five miles (40km) to the south-east, which reported in turn to the Leinster provincial meeting and the national meeting in Dublin. The Irish Quakers were excellent record keepers, which permits the historical reconstruction of the unique Ballymurray community over more than a century.

This study is very important to the local community of south Roscommon in particular. It examines records of daily life for a small community of Quakers, who for 130 years were substantial tenants of Lord Crofton of Mote Park. The Ballymurray community was sustained by their relationships with fellow Friends in Moate and elsewhere, but they must also be placed within the wider community in Co. Roscommon. They were closely connected to the local landowners, the Croftons, and appear to have been associated with the linen industry of south Roscommon.[5]

Mote Park was the seat of the Crofton family from the sixteenth century until the 1940s (fig. 2). The family owned over 11,000 acres (4,450ha) in Co. Roscommon in 1883; 7,000 of which were in the Mote Park estate.[6] Mote Park is now a Coillte-owned, 650-acre local amenity of woodland trails. Ballymurray is a typical rural townland that borders Mote Park to the east and which, up to the 1940s, was a scattered village 'boasting a railway station, post office, a dance hall, a forge, two shops and a village pump, all spread over two miles'.[7] In 1837, Samuel Lewis's *Topographical dictionary of Ireland* described Ballymurray as a village in the civil parish of Kilmeane in the barony

Introduction

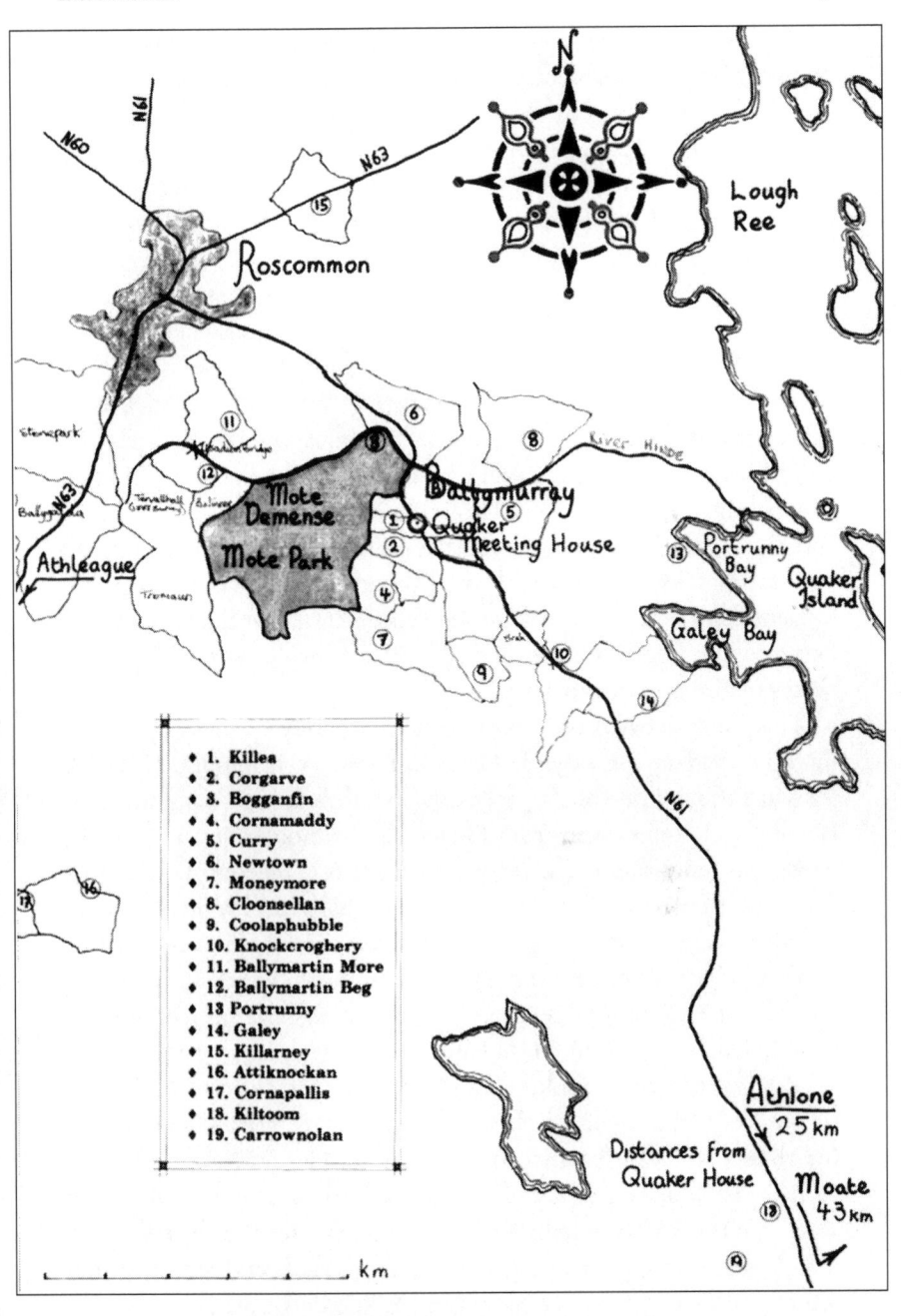

1. Killea
2. Corgarve
3. Bogganfin
4. Cornamaddy
5. Curry
6. Newtown
7. Moneymore
8. Cloonsellan
9. Coolaphubble
10. Knockcroghery
11. Ballymartin More
12. Ballymartin Beg
13. Portrunny
14. Galey
15. Killarney
16. Attiknockan
17. Cornapallis
18. Kiltoom
19. Carrownolan

2. Ballymurray Quaker meeting house and surrounds: map
(artwork by Maria May Fleming and Paul Cole; information compiled
by Jacqueline née Creaven d'Towey)

of Athlone of Co. Roscommon, just three miles (5km) south of the county town; it consisted at the time of several 'neatly built' houses and about twenty cabins.[8] Five years previously, Isaac Weld's *Statistical survey of County Roscommon* described Ballymurray as an 'ideal visual presentation' and he credited Quaker order and neatness to 'a spirit of improvement' that would have served Ireland well had it 'pervaded every part of this country'.[9]

Quakers in the Ballymurray area farmed just over 900 acres, as recorded in 1777 and 1828, making them sizable tenants of the Croftons of Mote Park and, importantly from the landlord's perspective, quality-improving tenants.[10] While the evidence is not plentiful, it appears that some of the first Quakers to arrive in Ballymurray came as linen workers and maintained a connection to proto-industry in the area.[11] The relationship between the Croftons and the local Quakers sometimes transcended the landlord–tenant connection. Links forged through marriage and friendship are evident from several sources, which demonstrate that the relationship between the Croftons and the Quakers was an important factor in their remaining in the locality.[12]

This book is based on a very substantial body of primary source material held in the Friends Historical Library in Dublin (FHLD). This includes minute books, memoirs, membership records, sufferings (accounts of tithes taken from Quakers), testimonies, journals, wills, deeds and genealogies. The records of the Moate meeting are essential sources as they contain detailed accounts of Ballymurray meetings and members. The Moate meeting records date from 1653 to 1856, with a small gap for the period 1822–33, although birth, marriage and death records for this period are extant. The records have been examined both in hard copy in the FHLD and in the electronic copies available on the website www.findmypast.co.uk. The Moate records are vast and reflect the diligence with which Quakers maintained documents for their own security and administration. The refusal of Quakers to take oaths or to pay tithes to the established church meant they were excluded from public office, university and the professions.[13] The Quakers therefore engaged in business, trade and manufacture, which produced a range of records including deeds, wills, memorials and lease agreements. The meeting records were kept to a set standard through a formula requiring each body to adhere to a set of queries. In

3. Mote Park house, June 1868 (courtesy of the Irish Architectural Archives). Mote Park was the home of Augusta Crofton Dillon (1839–1928) who married Luke Gerald Dillon of Clonbrock in 1866. Augusta is responsible for most of the images in the NLI Clonbrock Photographic Collection

a similar fashion, births, marriages and deaths/burials were recorded carefully, as were examples of new members who joined as a result of 'convincement'. While the records are detailed, they are limited in some respects. Monthly meetings noted those who had erred or who were diligent in living 'the Quaker way', but they paid infrequent attention to ordinary, less well-off members of the Society who gave no cause for concern.

As the main source for this work, the Quaker records are of major importance and offer unparalleled insight into the lives of a small minority of rural smallholders. The research also draws on a range of other sources. The Crofton Papers and Clonbrock Papers in the NLI have been used to assess Quaker links with the Crofton landlords and their interaction with Protestant neighbours.[14] The work of contemporary Quaker chroniclers and visitors provides some important insights into the Ballymurray community and their place within the wider Irish population of Quakers.[15] A 1746 list of Crofton tenants, along with the valuable census of the diocese of Elphin, undertaken by the Church of Ireland bishop Edward Synge in 1749, have been used to locate the Ballymurray Quakers in their neighbourhood in the mid-eighteenth century.[16]

The Ballymurray Quakers have not been the subject of sustained historical research, although Kenneth L. Carroll's 1979 essay 'Quakerism in Connacht, 1656–1978' provides a brief study from the Quaker perspective, which provided help in the identification of some dates and sources.[17] Carroll also published an essay on 'Quaker weavers of Newport, Ireland, 1720–40', a study of a Mayo Quaker settlement that moved to Ballymurray in the winter of 1739–40.[18] *The Crofton memoirs* give details of the Crofton family and some of their personalities along with details of estate management and improvements. This study has also drawn on the rich Quaker histories and guides to the Quaker records including Isabel Grubb's *Irish Quakers*, Olive C. Goodbody's *Irish Quaker records* and Maurice J. Wigham's *The Irish Quakers*.[19] Thomas Wight and John Rutty's *A history of the rise and progress of the people called Quakers in Ireland, from the year 1653–1750* provided little on Connacht Quakers but offered important context.[20] Biographies such as those of Alfred Webb, and Anna Haslam and Thomas Haslam highlighted the struggle of some Quakers to remain apolitical and pacifist.[21] Glynn Douglas's *Friends and 1798* provided accounts of Quaker concerns during this troubled period.[22] Hiram Wood's *Quakers of Limerick* located Edward Alexander after his departure from the Ballymurray Quakers in 1753, likewise Albert C. Myers's *Irish Quakers to Pennsylvania* documents those Quakers who left Ballymurray before 1760.[23]

The book is structured chronologically. Chapter 1 examines the period from 1717 to 1740. This assesses the arrival of the first Quakers in Ballymurray, their connection to the Croftons and the challenges they met during the subsequent two decades. After the collapse of the Newport, Co. Mayo, Quaker settlement in the harsh winter of 1739–40, the surviving Newport Quakers settled in the Ballymurray compass with the financial assistance of the Moate meeting. The book argues that although this was a significant boost to the number of members in the Ballymurray Quaker community, it also placed a heavy financial burden on them. The Ballymurray Quakers were not wealthy and held small holdings of between ten and fifteen acres. The exception was the Burne family of Galey who leased two holdings there amounting to over ninety acres. The period 1729–39 coincided with the deaths of two Lords Crofton, which also impacted on the progress of the Quaker community in Ballymurray.

The period 1741–88 is the subject of Chapter 2. The sources for these dates suggest a close-knit community with connections to the wider Protestant neighbouring population. This chapter demonstrates that the lack of suitable marriage partners negatively impacted on the growth in the population of the Ballymurray Quakers. This will be further explained within the social and economic conditions of the period and locality. Although Lord Marcus Lowther Crofton, who held his title from 1747 until his death in 1784, brought stability to the Crofton family, his tenure was marred by the high cost of a lengthy legal dispute over the ownership of Mote Park and the Crofton estate. Nearing the end of Marcus's term, his son Edward leased the property from his father and in 1777 a survey of the estate was carried out. This has been mined for information regarding the interactions between Crofton landlords and Quaker tenants.[24]

Chapter 3 discusses the final sixty years of the Ballymurray Quaker community to the discontinuance of the meeting in 1848. Six decades of decline led to the surrender of the lease of Ballymurray meeting house in 1858 to the Croftons. Several challenges were met in this period, beginning with the political polarization of the 1790s. Other challenges included insolvencies, inflation and insufficient means of livelihood. An ageing community and dwindling membership meant the future of the community was uncertain in the 1830s and 1840s. At the same time, the book shows that failure to retain members was a recurring and, ultimately, fatal problem for the Ballymurray community. Many former members remained in the area in the nineteenth century but, for various reasons, they no longer identified as Quakers.

Ultimately, the book demonstrates that the Quakers of Ballymurray deserve reflection and analysis, as a unique group of a religious minority, who resided in Connacht for a period of 130 years.

1. The beginning of the Ballymurray Quaker community, 1716–41

This chapter examines the origins and development of the Quaker community of Ballymurray, with a focus on the families who moved to Roscommon. The chapter draws on Quaker records and other sources to assess the economic and political contexts within which the Ballymurray Quaker settlement was established. Quaker records indicate the significance of Sir Edward Crofton of Mote Park, one of the most important landowners in Roscommon. They also provide important details concerning the first Quaker families to move to Ballymurray: the families of James Burne and Thomas Siggins who arrived from Sligo in early 1717.[1] The chapter also examines the case of another significant early arrival, Gershon Boate, who moved with his family to Ballymurray in 1718. Boate and his father, also called Gershon, had a connection with Crofton through their interactions with the Irish parliament. Crofton was an MP for Roscommon from 1703 until his death in 1729, while the elder Boate was an active Quaker lobbyist who attended many sittings of parliament.[2] Boate's father, the Dutch author and physician Gerard Boate, was reported 'to be acceptable to government and had an interest among, and a ready access to people in power', while Gershon was also a 'man to know'.[3] In 1718 Quaker colleagues turned to Gershon to assist with the acquisition of land in Ballymurray for a meeting house and burial ground.[4] This chapter begins by assessing the origins of the community between 1716 and 1728, before examining the developments of the period from 1729 to 1738 and, finally, the arrival of a number of Quakers from a defunct community in Newport, Co. Mayo. The chapter charts the history of the community by examining births, marriages and deaths. The small community was challenged by prevailing social and economic conditions, notably the food shortages of 1725–9 and the catastrophic famine of 1739–41.[5]

The beginning of the Ballymurray Quaker community, 1716–41

Quakers arrived in Ballymurray in search of improved opportunities, work and possibly land, as part of a voluntary movement, but one somewhat forced by social and economic circumstances. In the latter decades of the seventeenth century and the early eighteenth century, Quakers faced persecution in Ireland. This included imprisonment for non-payment of tithes, exclusion from Ireland's sole university (Trinity College Dublin) and lack of compensation settlements in cases of damage or being burnt out of their homes.[6] James Burne and Thomas Siggins, the first Quakers to arrive in Ballymurray, were in immediate need of land, having had 'their land sold over their heads', as Quaker records put it, suggesting the sale of their land was against their will.[7]

The Burne and Siggins families arrived from 'near' Sligo in mid-1717 and had been the subject of legal proceedings in the local Sligo ecclesiastical (Church of Ireland) court.[8] It is not known from precisely where in Sligo the Burne and Siggins families arrived, but Wight and Rutty make a vague reference to Sligo and 'Scarnegirah'.[9] James Burne and Thomas Siggins, along with James's brother George, had spent the previous eighteen months back and forth between Sligo gaol, the bishop's court (an ecclesiastical court) and the sheriff in a dispute over their testimony against tithes. In all they were said to have each spent almost six months in gaol. The Quaker communities in Dublin and Moate, as well as the Croftons of Mote Park, assisted the Burne and Siggins families, resulting in their release from prison.[10] Several letters, enquiries and reports relating to their dispute, from the period 1716–18, mention Sir Edward Crofton and his son Edward Crofton, and they leased land to the Burne and Siggins families in Galey (along the western shore of Lough Ree).[11] By November 1717, Leinster Friends reported at the national half-yearly meeting in Dublin that those who had lived near Sligo and had removed to Roscommon had not yet settled to their satisfaction. 'It was desired of' the Leinster province to keep them in their care and see them comfortably settled, 'in faithfulness to their convincement'.[12] At the next national half-yearly meeting of May 1718, it was reported that the Quaker Friends in Roscommon had settled, and had been joined by several other families from 'divers' parts of Ireland.[13]

The Quakers who arrived from Sligo settled at or near Ballymurray (which some referred to as Marystown), three miles

(5km) from Roscommon town and ten miles (16km) from Athlone. They were joined by several other Quaker families who moved to Ballymurray from Mountrath and Mountmellick meetings and many were inter-related through marriage. The Quaker families that settled in Roscommon were listed as farming lands on the Crofton estate of Mote Park and were noted in the Quaker records as having had tithes collected from them in 1719.[14] The earliest Quaker list of tithes, collected in the civil parishes of Kilmeane and Killinvoy, Co. Roscommon, for 1719, recorded eight names. This allows us to identify and locate the initial members of the community. They included Gershon Boate, Robert Sinklar and Henry Wilson of Kilmeane parish. James and George Burne (brothers) with Thomas Siggins, John White and Henry Fuller farmed in the parish of Killinvoy.[15] Records suggest that John White and Henry Fuller farmed but did not live in Ballymurray.

John White married Agnes Knott in Edenderry on 14 May 1717. No birth records for this couple have been found. Agnes's death and burial in 1781 were recorded in Monasteroris civil parish near Edenderry, suggesting that the couple did not reside in Ballymurray.[16] Henry Fuller, a nephew-in-law of Gershon Boate, had tithes taken for land in Roscommon for the years 1719–21. He was the son of Jacob and Jane Fuller of Waterstown, Co. Westmeath, and married Deborah Barcroft in May 1718. He requested a certificate to move to Carlow in September 1717.[17] The evidence for Henry Fuller indicates that he was an absentee grazier and that he sublet grazing land in this area, as suggested by the tithes he had confiscated (no crops, just lambs and fleeces).[18] The origins of Ballymurray Quaker community therefore involved just six families, most related either by marriage or blood.

The individuals mentioned above were recorded in the book of 'sufferings' (goods distrained, as tithes collected) in 1719.[19] The tithes of that year, collected from their farms, included lambs, fleeces and harvested crops (wheat, oats, barley, beer, beans, peas and flax) to the value of £27 4s. 1d.[20] The small community would have required stability, support and opportunity in order to prosper, especially as it faced successive challenges in the early decades of its existence. The community was connected, particularly through the Jackson female line. Mary Jackson, who married Robert Sinklar, was probably a cousin of Rebecca Jackson, wife of Gershon Boate (marriage records indicate that John and Robert were, respectively, the fathers of Mary and Rebecca).[21] Boate was an important figure in the early community. Born in 1678, he was the son of another Gershon Boate and the grandson of Gerard Boate, as noted above a prominent figure in mid-seventeenth-century Ireland.[22] Gershon (born 1678) married Rebecca Jackson in Mountmellick on 23 October 1700, and they later moved from Mountmellick to Ballymurray with their six children. On 16 July 1718 the Moate monthly men's meeting noted that Gershon should be contacted in order 'to set out a convenient place in Ballymurray land for a burying place and a place to build a meeting house on'.[23] The site chosen for this purpose was at the juncture of three townlands: Ballymurray, Corgarve and Killea.[24] A meeting house was constructed at the edge of the Crofton estate of Mote Park, on land which appears to have been leased on favourable terms (a renewal was sought in 1773), as an incentive or perhaps a reward for the Quaker community's presence.[25] The Croftons were improving landlords, as indicated by their commitment to the Ballymurray Quaker community. They were involved in politics, agriculture and current affairs, and committed to the survival of their estate and industrious tenants who leased land on their estate. In the 1720s both Sir Edward Crofton, 2nd baronet, and his son Edward served as MPs for Roscommon County as well as on the Irish Privy Council and both were trustees of the Linen Board in 1721.[26]

Ballymurray Quaker meeting house was built c.1721, measuring twenty-three feet by fifteen feet.[27] The building survives and there is evidence in the remaining plaster on the walls to suggest the location of the minister's gallery at the eastern gable, as well as a fireplace in the western gable. As David M. Butler notes, 'the small country meeting house at Ballymurray is most unusual in having a fireplace in the meeting room itself'.[28] The surviving evidence suggests a well-built quality structure constructed by craftsmen. In the same year, a Quaker community built a meeting house in Wicklow. The quarterly Leinster province minutes indicate that funds were raised for the construction, with subscriptions called for from the meetings of Moate, Carlow, Dublin, Mountmellick and Waterford, all under the care of Leinster.[29] A total of £145 was raised over an eighteen-month period. The only contemporary Quaker records for the construction of a meeting house in Ballymurray is a single sentence in the Leinster minutes of 1722. This stated that a meeting house was built at 'Marys Town' (Marystown was probably an Anglicized corruption of the Gaelic name Baile Uí Mhuirígh / Ballymurray) and two records of payments, one of £4 made to Gershon Boate and another of £1 10s. 8½d. 'paid Connacht Friends towards building of their meeting house at Ballymurray'.[30] The lack of other references (for example, the kind of fundraising that occurred in the case of Wicklow) suggests that the building at Ballymurray was funded by a third party, probably Sir Edward Crofton. Later in the eighteenth century, the Croftons used incentives or rewards to attract what they considered industrious tenants. In 1784 *Faulkner's Dublin Journal* carried an advertisement in which (a later) Sir Edward Crofton called for Protestant workers to move to Ballymurray to work locally in the linen industry, noting that houses would be built for them. Two years earlier, an Edward Burne of Galey was offered very cheap rent, an incentive for his 'service on all and any occasion to Mr Crofton'.[31] In the absence of direct evidence, it is possible to suggest that this kind of incentivization had also been in operation in the 1720s and that the Ballymurray meeting house was one consequence. The quality of the building suggests that it was not built by the Quakers themselves (modesty and function were more suited to Quaker architecture). This is borne out by comparison with other meeting houses, notably the one in Moate, which was in constant need of repair; in the period 1710–17 alone, eight repairs were recorded.[32] In 1767–8 it was razed to the ground and rebuilt, only to undergo further repairs within ten years. Ballymurray meeting house, in contrast, was repaired infrequently, such as in 1804, possibly in anticipation of the American Jesse Kersey's visit.[33]

In the early 1720s, Sir Edward Crofton, 2nd baronet of the Mote, was one of the leading figures in Co. Roscommon, and he owned an estate of 11,000 acres. As noted above, in 1721 he was a trustee of the Irish Linen Board and an MP for Roscommon; in the same year Edward Crofton (most probably related to Sir Edward), John Pratt and Edward Southwell were fellow trustees.[34] It is likely that Crofton promoted the Quaker community in Ballymurray for reasons of improvement, as it was in his interest to provide employment, or tenants of means, for his estate. Isaac Weld's *Statistical survey of*

County Roscommon, published in 1832, described Mote Park as 'a little district [that] commands notice for the neatness of the cottages, and the excellent quickset hedges. It was formally inhabited almost exclusively by Quakers'. As Carroll noted in his 1979 article 'Quaker weavers of Newport', Benjamin Holme reported in 1725 that

> many very considerable men in this country, that have great quantities of land to set, do very much covet to have Friends (Society of Friends) for their tenants; for many of our Friends have been so diligent and industrious, and have made such fine improvements upon the farms that they have taken, and have also been so punctual in paying their rents, that they are very much respected by their landlords.[35]

The practice of recruiting Protestant workers for the linen and yarn industry was not unusual. Robert French of Monivea provides an important example that is well documented.[36] In another well-known case, Sir Thomas Southwell of Limerick settled a community of Palatine migrants on his estate in 1709. The promotion of the linen industry had been attempted elsewhere in the early eighteenth century. It is even possible that Crofton's patronage of the Quaker community at Ballymurray was an attempt to emulate Southwell, but on a much smaller scale.[37] It is significant too that the Linen Board, established in 1711, invested heavily in Co. Roscommon during its first decade. The board spent £584 3s. 6d. on the promotion of the linen and linen yarn industry in the county (linen yarn was easier to produce, requiring less labour and time, before it was sold on to finishers), more than in any other Connacht county, including Galway, which received £540.[38] Unfortunately, direct contemporary evidence for Crofton's involvement in Ballymurray is slim, but the link remained in local memory and was recorded in the school's folklore collection in the early twentieth century. Local memory of a connection between Crofton and linen production was preserved by a schoolteacher residing next to the Ballymurray meeting house, who possessed a one-hundred-year-old locally produced linen tablecloth.[39]

Growth of the Ballymurray Quaker community during the early decades of its existence was slow and interrupted on two occasions by the deaths of Sir Edward Crofton, 2nd baronet, in November 1729 and

Sir Edward Crofton, 3rd baronet, of the Mote in November 1739.[40] Life cycle events – births, marriages and deaths – provide some sense of the development of the community. The period 1729–39 produced four marriages but only one birth. The baby was Gershon Boate, who died aged five weeks in August 1731, followed by his mother, Mary, nine days later. Nine deaths were recorded for the years 1729 to 1738, two from the Sinklar family, three from the Boate family and four from the Burne family. George Burne (brother of James, the early settler from Sligo) died in 1729. He was the young husband of Abigail Jackson and father to the infant, Judith. George and Abigail had married in 1726 in Mountrath but resided in Newtown, Co. Roscommon. Their marriage was one of the earliest associated with Ballymurray and would have encouraged the fledgling community. After George's death Abigail and her daughter moved away from the community when she married for a second time to William Walpole of Mountrath in April 1732.[41] The first of the four marriages to take place in Ballymurray in this period was that of Richard Church of Dublin to Deborah Wilson (daughter of Henry Wilson) in 1728. Deborah died within two years of marriage, resulting in Richard migrating to Pennsylvania.[42] The marriage of Deborah and Richard Church illustrates several of the problems faced by Ballymurray Quakers: the decline in numbers due to early death, lack of prospects for those new to the area with no land and the hard-to-quantify impact of dashed or lost hopes. Of the three other marriages in Ballymurray during this decade, none were to survive as Quaker marriages with Quaker children. This is evident from the 1749 Census of Elphin and from Quaker records. The reasons suggested in the Quaker records are complex and include marriage to a 'papist' on the death of a Quaker spouse; disownment for abandoning wife and family; running up debts; frequenting ale houses and not keeping to his word, as was the case for one Richard Nevitt.[43] The community disowned one couple for absconding to a different country after running up debts and keeping scandalous company while maintaining a 'tippling-house'.[44] The very rules that portrayed Quakers as honest, peaceful, upright people excluded many Quakers through the means of disownment and disunity from Quaker membership as a result of breaking those rules. Indeed, the evidence suggests a lack of leniency in the interpretation of the rules during the early decades of the Ballymurray community. For example, Gershon Boate junior and Jonathan Robinson, both widowers with young children, were disowned for marrying out of the Quaker denomination. While Quaker marriages in Ballymurray suggest that the community was developing in the late 1720s and 1730s, this was not really the case and the community struggled as a result. The diminishing numbers must have placed pressure on the community, which helps to explain why it welcomed a group of Newport Quakers in the very difficult winter of 1739–40.

The family of Henry Wilson was among the first to settle in Ballymurray and their case is illustrative of the concerns and struggles of the community in its early phase. Among the issues the community faced was an absence of suitable marriage partners, lack of prospects resulting in migration and non-adherence to the Quaker rules, which could lead to expulsion from the community. Henry Wilson married Mary Heaton in early 1705 and moved in 1718 from the civil parish of Kilkenny West on the Leinster side of Lough Ree to Ballymurray. Henry and Mary had five daughters born between 1706 and 1715. Quaker records suggest that Henry had a quick temper. One source described him as a man 'to give way to passion as to give a Joseph Knott a blow with a switch on being provoked with foul language'.[45] This suggests a man of strong beliefs, even a man under strain. It might be significant that he had no son, or son-in-law, to share his workload; his first daughter did not marry until 1728 (Deborah to Richard Church). The evidence of tithes taken in 1711 and 1713 in Co. Westmeath suggests that Henry grew crops including oats, barley, peas and beans. He continued this practice in Ballymurray, where he farmed eighty acres under abatement to Gershon Boate and Robert Sinklar.[46] Problems arose in 1726, as detailed in many minutes of the Moate men's meeting. Henry and Mary Wilson were involved in a dispute with the two Gershon Boates, father and son, in part concerning the eighty acres of Ballymurray that Henry farmed. The dispute appears to have involved the rate or value given to the land and improvements carried out on the farm.[47] The dispute was not resolved and continued after Henry's death some time in 1727 when Mary, his widow, took Gershon senior to court for neglect of duties as executor of her late husband's will.[48] Carroll stated incorrectly that Mary married again, to a Richard Nevitt, in 1730. In fact, Mary's daughter, Elizabeth, married Nevitt, who was from Dublin. In 1735, the Moate meeting was supporting Mary Heaton, most probably Henry Wilson's widow, to the value of £2 10s.[49] She was also referred to as 'Old Mary Heaton'. In 1739 a Joseph Nephit was willing to pay Richard Nevitt on account of maintenance of Mary Heaton, Richard's mother-in-law.[50] This was followed in 1741 by a payment of £1 made by James Burne junior to Richard Nevitt for Mary's upkeep. The difficulties faced by Henry Wilson's family were not uncommon, as is clear from other developments within the community.

Their circumstances varied according to their possession of land, the strength of their support (usually a male relative) and their age or suitability to remarry and produce children. Mary Wilson née Heaton's case against Gershon Boate, father and son, in 1726–7 appears to have gone against Mary who received financial support from fellow Friends into her old age. Reluctantly, land was sometimes divided, as in the case of George Burne's widow Abigail and her inheritance; the Burne family were praised for their generosity.[51] The executors of George Burne's will were Robert Sinklar, Abigail's brother-in-law, and James Burne, her father-in-law. A dispute over this will continued from March 1729 until December 1731. Abigail Burne was a young widow and remarried in 1732 to a William Walpole and moved from Ballymurray. She may have been given a monetary value for the land she inherited as it remained in the hands of identifiable Ballymurray Quakers. The marriage of Richard Church of Athy, Co. Kildare, who served his time as an apprentice shoemaker, and Deborah Wilson, daughter of Henry Wilson and Mary Heaton, took place on 27 June 1728 in Ballymurray Quaker meeting house and was clearly an important occasion. Thirty-six named witnesses attended, including four Wilsons (all female, suggesting that Henry Wilson, the bride's father, had died by this stage, a point reinforced by his absence from the marriage certificate), six Boates, seven Burnes, two Nevitts, one Siggins and five Sinklars.[52] Deborah died, however, within a year. By May 1729 Richard was described as a widower on his certificate for removal for Pennsylvania. He settled in Buckingham County, where he was received on 4 November 1729.[53] Early deaths must have shaken the small community, especially while enduring the poor harvests of 1725–9. These years saw food shortages and financial hardship across Ireland, which impacted the Quaker communities in Connacht.

Disputes among the Quakers of Ballymurray illustrate further difficulties faced by the small community. Gershon Boate senior was involved in up to a dozen court cases, some as defendant, others as complainant, some with family members including his children, and some involving several Quakers in cases similar to a class action. When disputes arose, the Quakers of Ballymurray tended to resolve their differences with the assistance of the men's meeting in Moate, often involving a series of enquiries and on-site visits. If this form of mediation failed, it appears that they took their cases to the court of chancery or court of exchequer in Dublin. Gershon Boate and Mrs Wilson, a widow, did just this in 1727.[54] Gershon was an executor of Henry Wilson's will and was faulted for his tardiness in the execution of his duties.[55]

Indeed, the difficulties faced by the Boate family ultimately led to their disownment and the loss of the entire Boate family to the Ballymurray Quaker community by 1737. The eldest of Gershon's children, another Gershon, was born in 1701, and 'he took to wife' Mary Godwin or Godin of Mountmellick in 1721. By 1733 Gershon the younger was a butcher, widower and father of three young girls: Mary, Hannah and Rachel (born between 1723 and 1726).[56] In 1726–7 Gershon the younger was involved in a dispute with his father over a large sum of money. In 1729 he had a condemnation paper read against him for shooting his landlord's sow. In 1735 he was disowned 'for his odious and scandalous actions with a servant maid of his, and he now intending to marry her'; she was not a Quaker.[57] Gershon was probably the same butcher who sold veal to the Glass family, as mentioned in a household account of 1733–4 for a property near Knockcroghery.[58] The same account also recorded a Rachel Boate and Samuel Boate. Rachel sold 'Hopps' and Samuel 'a fat cow' worth £2 6s. Gershon Boate senior moved to Edenderry between 1729 and 1732, but returned in 1736 to Ballymurray, where he was testified against and taken to court for striking a neighbour. In 1739 he too was disowned.[59] Rachel Boate and her brother Samuel were also disowned in September 1735 for running up debt in a business their father had settled upon them.[60] They absconded to England without paying creditors.[61] Rachel returned to set up a new business, ignored her creditors and married a Catholic, Andrew Ross, and for this reason she was disowned again in September 1742.[62] The case of Rachel

Boate and her second disownment is one of the first examples of 'forgiveness' and reuniting in the Ballymurray Quaker community; some level of reacceptance as a Quaker had clearly occurred before her second disownment in 1742.

The years 1739–41 witnessed crucial developments in the early history of the Ballymurray community. The death of Sir Edward Crofton, 3rd baronet, on 11 November 1739 had implications for lessees and caused uncertainty at a difficult time. The most significant crisis of the century in Ireland also began in the late winter of 1739 when seven weeks of frost and sub-zero temperatures led to rivers freezing, while potatoes stored in the ground turned to mush. This caused the famine of 1740–1.[63] Roscommon was affected in the same manner as the rest of the country in 1739–41, particularly by the crisis brought on by extreme weather conditions. It is significant that in the context of the ongoing national crises, a group of Quakers from Newport, Co. Mayo, settled in Ballymurray in this period. Carroll suggested that their arrival bolstered the Ballymurray community.[64] Yet when considering the history of the Newport Quakers, who had endured challenges almost continually since their arrival there in 1721, it seems more sensible to view Ballymurray as a refuge for the new arrivals. The Newport Quakers were originally weavers from Rathfriland, Co. Down, as well as from Drogheda, Co. Louth. They had moved to Newport to engage in the linen industry under the establishment of Captain John Pratt, who was listed as a trustee of the Linen Board in 1721.[65] James Kelly has noted that Ireland was short of cash in spring 1725 and Pratt, who was deputy vice-treasurer, owed the exchequer nearly £75,000.[66] This was particularly pertinent to the Newport Quakers who as early as 1720 had been advised by the Dublin monthly meeting 'to be very careful how they take up money from Captain Pratt, and be frugal and sparing in laying out money either on building or otherwise'.[67] The Newport Quakers experienced a series of difficulties in the later 1720s including deaths, both of children and of adults, the disownment of John Cantrell due to mismanagement of business and breach of trust in 1727, lack of paid work and disorderly behaviour such as drinking and swearing, which were also causes for disownment.[68] By 1729 several of the Newport Quakers had emigrated to America, including the Evans and McClung/McClunn families.[69] In 1735–6, £60 of interest-free capital had been raised by fellow Quakers to support the Newport weavers to keep their looms at work.[70] From the earliest years in Mayo, the Quakers struggled and the final laying-down of the Newport meeting occurred in the late winter and spring of 1739–40, when the few remaining families moved to the Ballymurray Quaker community. According to Carroll, this greatly helped sustain the Ballymurray Quakers, yet financial support was necessary for some of those who moved. Families who arrived from Newport included Sutcliff, Peck, McGaw, McLean and Heannan. The minutes of Moate men's meetings suggest that those of Roscommon faced a similar recovery period as the rest of the country, following the 1740–1 famine. After her removal to Moate, widow Sutcliff, relict of William, who had tithes taken in Mayo in 1723, received financial support. So too did Nathan Nevitt, who received monies for the necessities for a poor widow Peck in Ballymurray (Mrs Peck and her husband John had moved from Mayo in 1739–40).[71]

The beginnings of the Ballymurray Quaker community had been beset with difficulties; very little if anything had been easy. Local support for this fledgling community was interrupted by the loss of two lords Crofton in 1729 and 1739. The hardships of famine, poor harvests, severe weather, death and illness, along with the financial shortages of the country and its ability to support proto-industry in distant parts of the country disadvantaged this micro-community in Connacht. The period of 1717 to 1741 saw very little increase in Quaker numbers, and it is testament to their tenacity that they survived for another one hundred years.

2. Ballymurray Quakers and their locality, 1741–88

By the early 1740s the Quaker community in Ballymurray had endured a series of challenges and, over the succeeding decades, the community developed and in turn produced more records from which their history can be reconstructed. This chapter assesses the crucial period from the 1740s to the end of the 1780s, before the impact of radical politics in the 1790s would present a new set of challenges. To begin, the chapter examines the nature of the community and its relationships with the people in the locality through a number of key sources. The first is a list of local people who are recorded on a document related to the legal case of Oliver Crofton versus Marcus Lowther Crofton in 1746–7, which contested title ownership to Mote Park and the Crofton estate. The second is the census of the diocese of Elphin carried out under the Church of Ireland bishop Edward Synge in 1749. The Quakers on the list of 1746–7 will be compared to those named on the census undertaken two years later, and further comparisons will be made to the Quakers who were recorded as attached to the Ballymurray meeting. The records illustrate the dependence of the middling sort, educated Quakers on their neighbours, including local Church of Ireland landlords.

This chapter outlines the challenges faced by the community and the manner in which the Quakers responded. Marriage remained a major difficulty for the community, which was simply too small in an area of few opportunities for advancement to provide a sufficient number of potential partners. Education and the apprentice system of the Ballymurray Quakers is also examined, drawing on the work of Leanne Calvert and Mary O'Dowd. The chapter outlines the impact of losing elderly members, especially James Burne and Thomas Siggins, as well as declining numbers due to migration and the search for employment. The many stresses faced by Quakers of Ballymurray from the 1740s to the 1780s were marked by their relationship with the wider community and the Croftons of Mote Park. The challenges fostered resilience, however, and the Quaker community adapted their rules in order to survive, for example by offering leniency to members who expressed 'sorrow for their transgression'. A propensity to pursue affluent members, and those who may have absented themselves, is demonstrated in the cases of the Sproules and Burnes. Carroll suggested that the Ballymurray Quaker community reached its zenith by the 1780s, with decline setting in before the end of the eighteenth century. This chapter argues that the decline commenced in the 1750s and continued, despite the efforts of the community, at a slow pace throughout the remainder of the century.

There are two valuable contemporary sources that provide details of the local population in the 1740s. The first is the list of one hundred supporters (notice parties) of Marcus Lowther Crofton in the 1746/7 case of Crofton versus Crofton, a case eventually won by Marcus.[1] The second is the Synge census of Elphin of 1749.[2] The two sources demonstrate just how small the Quaker community was and this helps to explain the necessity of their reliance on the surrounding Protestant population for marriage and economic opportunities. Quaker numbers were simply too small to survive independently without adapting or conforming to the surrounding conditions. The fact that they survived for 130 years is testament to their adjustment as a micro-community within the locality.

The list of supporters in the case Oliver Crofton v. Marcus Lowther Crofton is recorded in a bill book of Chancery dated 1746/7. The case involved the contested (alleged to have been forged) will of Sir Edward Crofton, 4th baronet, who died without issue in March 1745. As noted in Chapter 1, the first and second baronets had died in 1729 and 1739, so that the death in 1745 of the 4th baronet heralded the third change of ownership of Mote Park and a potentially destabilizing influence on the small Quaker community.[3] The 4th baronet, like his father and grandfather, had been an MP for Roscommon and he had served with the British Army. He died near Tournai, in modern Belgium, shortly before the Battle of Fontenoy. An early twentieth-century family history, *The Crofton memoirs*, claimed that he had, in fact, died at Mote on 25 March 1745. In any case, the 4th baronet was in possession of the Mote Park estate for only six years. A legal battle between Oliver Crofton (a practising barrister at the time) and Marcus Lowther Crofton, brother-in-law to the deceased 4th baronet, followed for title of Mote Park and the Crofton estate. Marcus won the case and was granted title to Mote Park estate but, in his own words recorded in a family bible, it was a 'long and vexatious lawsuit'. It was also a costly event that put a financial strain on Marcus Lowther Crofton.[4] Seeking local support, Marcus and Oliver had advertised in several newspapers of their willingness to offer favourable tenure to those who continued their leases with Mote Park; in one, Marcus confirmed his 'support and defence' of existing tenants.[5] The chancery bill book list contained one hundred names, sixty-two of whom also appeared in the 1749 census of Elphin, including three from the Boate family, who were disowned Quakers, as well as six Quakers from the Ballymurray meeting. Of the remaining names, eighteen have not been identified by this author, while the remainder have been identified using contemporary sources. Six were Crofton relatives who were not named on the 1749 census. This list suggests that the Quaker community was very small, but that they were part of the propertied or business people of the local community. As a result of the solidarity they showed to Marcus Lowther Crofton, they secured favourable conditions that made survival more certain, most probably by and for the individual, but to the benefit of the small group of inter-related families.

In the census of Elphin, ten townlands were chosen for close examination based on their association with Quaker families recorded in the records of the Moate meeting. These ten townlands were Attiknockan, Ballymurray, Bogganfin, Cornamaddy, Coolaphubble, Galey, Galey Beg, Killarney, Mote Demesne and Newtown. The total number of households recorded for these townlands was eighty-seven, of which thirty-three were 'Protestant', four were 'Quaker' (the only Quaker households recorded in the census) and the remaining fifty were 'Catholic'.[6] At 58 per cent, the proportion of Catholics in these ten townlands was lower than in the census as a whole. The census recorded a total of 15,099 Catholic households accounting for 89.6 per cent.[7] Of the thirty-three Protestant households enumerated in the ten townlands, four households in Newtown were recorded as 'Protestant' although those living there were active members of the Quaker community at that time according to the minutes of Moate men's monthly meeting. The census recorded John Nevitt, William Nevitt and John McGaw, all weavers, and James Burne, a farmer, all residing in Newtown in the civil parish of Kiltoom, as 'Protestant'.[8] This may have been a decision of the church warden who enumerated the townland, perhaps an attempt to enhance his congregation numbers. A similar pattern is evident in the townland of Killarney in the civil parish of Roscommon, where two families named Heanon, both weavers, were recorded as 'Protestant', but were, in fact, Quakers. Jonathan Robinson of Killarney was listed as a 'Protestant' with ten children under the age of fourteen. Both Jonathan and some of his children would be disunited and re-admitted to the Quakers in the years that followed. The description of these seven Quaker households in the census figures of 1749 illustrates the bias or inaccuracies that occurred in collecting the information. The census of Elphin does illustrate one very important point, however: that the Quakers of Ballymurray resided in areas with a higher proportion of 'Protestant' neighbours than the remainder of the diocese of Elphin. If all of the Quaker households had been correctly identified in the census of Elphin, the ten townlands examined had 13 per cent Quaker, 29 per cent Protestant and 58 per cent Catholic households.

Quaker marriages recorded in Ballymurray between the 1740s and the 1780s offer some insight into the sustainability and growth of the group. The ability or failure of the Ballymurray community to sustain Quaker-to-Quaker marriages and the reliance on the larger Protestant congregation for marriage partners is evident in the contemporary records. For the Quakers, marriage was a serious business governed by many rules and conditions peculiar to their denomination, deviation from which was usually met with disunity or disownment from the Society of Friends. Quakers viewed all members as equal, so they did not require priests, nor did they recognize sacraments. Legalizing a Quaker marriage in the eyes of the state meant that it was to be performed in a registered meeting house, witnessed by a minimum of twelve persons.[9] It is unclear when Ballymurray meeting house was registered but the first Ballymurray wedding took place in 1724 at Moate, and 1728 saw the first marriage in Ballymurray meeting house, so it may be assumed that the date of the meeting house registration was between 1724 and 1728. Before the 1850s, Quakers were expected to marry a partner from within their own denomination.

Requirements for Quaker marriage included the consent of parents before approaching the prospective spouse, two public declarations of intention to marry and, finally, a report by senior Quakers as to the freedom of the prospective spouses from other marriages or any cause why they could not marry.[10] Marriages among the Ballymurray Quakers, constrained by these rules, also appear to have conformed to certain marriage traditions and customs not specific to Quakers such as the bride's residence as marriage location, the bride taking the groom's name and adherence to rules of consanguinity.

Between 1720 and 1834, fifty-two Quaker marriages with Ballymurray connections were recorded and, of those, only fifteen were celebrated in Ballymurray meeting house. The first took place in 1728 and the final Ballymurray Quaker marriage occurred on 18 December 1834. It was that of William Odlum and Hannah Fairbrother.[11] The fifteen Ballymurray weddings were outnumbered by the many marriages in which the Quaker spouse married a person of a different denomination or 'married out'. The scarcity of potential Quaker life partners and the strong character needed to choose marriage over denomination are demonstrated in the case of Elizabeth Goff. Goff was disowned in 1760 for 'marrying out', and she subsequently refused to meet Friends 'if it was about her marriage, which she did not deny nor repent and would do so again'.[12] Most marriages to non-Quakers led to the disownment of the Quaker spouse, reducing an already small community and contributing to its eventual demise. Thirty-two disownments of Ballymurray Quakers were recorded for the years between 1740 and 1788. Eighteen involved members of the community who were disowned for marrying outside the society. Of these, three people were disowned for marrying Catholics. Two disownments occurred in consequence of elopements without parental consent, while one happened on account of abduction. One woman was accused of having a child outside marriage (described as 'whoredom') and one man was disowned for getting a servant pregnant (the phrase used to describe him was that he 'dirtied himself'). The remaining six disownments resulted from cases of fraud, debt and quarrelling that led to abandonment.[13]

Many issues affected Quaker marriages in Ballymurray and, in consequence, the membership of the local community. Those to have a negative impact included abandonment of spouses and children, fraudulent accounts of financial status, running up debt, failing to pay creditors, pre-marital sex and violence, as well as elopement and abduction. Violent abduction of young single women happened in rural Ireland, and one such occurrence was recorded in 1770 in Galey, Roscommon.[14] The case, which involved members of the Ballymurray meeting, was documented in the testimonies of denial at Moate meetings in 1770.[15] On 1 March 1770 a letter of denial and public testimony was drawn up against Thomas Robinson of Killarney on account of his 'evil and scandalous actions' and 'the trampling of the wholesome rules among us in the weighty affair of marriage'. Thomas, who had twice been refused permission to court Nathan Nevitt's daughter, Elizabeth, had arrived at her uncle's house in Galey where the young lady was staying. He came with several armed men 'in a wicked, clandestine and audacious manner where he did forcibly take her out of said uncle's house'. The young Miss Nevitt avoided the abduction after her aunt, who ran to neighbours to raise the alarm, had been fired on by pistol, and this caused the abductors to flee the scene. Thomas Robinson wrote a letter of apology dated 3 September 1773, which was evidently accepted for he was deemed free to marry Elizabeth Alexander, daughter of George, on 12 November 1773 in Ballymurray meeting house.[16] Thomas and Elizabeth Robinson settled in Killarney where they had seven daughters and two sons between 1775 and 1791.[17]

Quaker records suggest that readmission, sometimes including forgiveness, was a common experience in Ballymurray. It could be suggested that this was due to the pressure to retain members, or to acquire new members through the birth of children to marriages of one Quaker spouse who had previously been disowned.[18] One intriguing case, which did not entirely illustrate this point but demonstrated a desire to maintain connections with the wealthier Quaker families, was that of Sarah Burne and her half-uncle Edward Burne who had eloped to an island on the Shannon, for which they were both disowned in 1749.[19] The unnamed island mentioned in the source was most likely Inchcleraun, locally known as Quaker Island, where an Edward Fairbrother held a lease from a Lady Featherstone in the late 1700s.[20] In 1755 Judith Burne and John Fairbrother, both Quakers, married in Ballymurray. They had six children all born in

Newtown, Co. Roscommon; their son Edward resided for a time with his wife Hannah née Parvin on Inchcleraun.[21] Both the Burne and Fairbrother names, as well as 'Quaker Island', were prominent in Ballymurray Quaker records until the 1820s. Local memory is familiar with Quaker Island but almost bereft of any recollection of the Quaker community from whence it was named. Adapting to survive, many of the Quakers in Ballymurray were 'in and out' of Quaker membership, which may explain their oversight in local memory, because many appear to have been absorbed by the local Protestant population.

Quakers assumed that the early education of children was the responsibility of women. In most meetings there was a separate women's monthly meeting and its role included care of the sick and poor, as well as the moral guidance of children and servants, to encompass speech and dress.[22] Quaker women held their own monthly meetings for business, but very few minutes from women's monthly meetings are extant. Just one minute book (MS H.23) for Moate, which covers the years 1798–1819 (considered in the next chapter) and 1846–74 (by which point Ballymurray Quaker meeting had ceased to exist), survives.[23] Moate had a separate building known as the 'Little meeting house', which was for the use of the women's monthly meeting and their business. Several minutes of the Moate men's monthly meeting mentioned their women's meeting, including the purchase of a 'seat with a back on it for women in said Little meeting house' in 1735.[24] Biannually, during the national half-yearly meetings held in Dublin, education and guidance for the children, youth and servants was discussed, and minutes for these are extensive.[25] One of the queries, number thirty-five, set forth at the November 1732 national half-yearly meeting was: 'do Friends take care of poor Friends due care of, and do their children partake of necessary learning to fit them for trades, and are they advised to put them forth as apprentices or servants'.[26] Planning and foresight in relation to education and family size were evident in school and apprenticeship records.[27] Consideration for the future profession of Quaker adult children, and the careful consideration for the relief of pressures on household circumstances by reducing numbers of dependants, was also planned. One such case was that of Robert Heaton and his wife who were advised by Moate meeting to lessen their family by putting their children to service, as recorded on 25 April 1716 at Moate men's monthly meeting.[28]

Little documentation exists in the Quaker archive to confirm whether any formal education took place in Ballymurray during the first half of the eighteenth century. John Walby and John Little, both schoolmasters, resided in Moate in the 1750s, suggesting that some families could employ private educators for their children.[29] Letters, pamphlets, guides and books introduced ideas for learning, and young people were advised to attend book readings and special meetings to ensure that the Quaker doctrine was promoted.[30] Literature that was deemed acceptable by the Quakers was often recorded in the minute books, including the cost of such publications and the number of books ordered by each meeting.[31] One such order highlighted the Quaker commercial sensibilities; when ordering *Piety promoted* in 1721, the cost per book was 3s. 6d. with a seventh copy free.[32] Moate placed an order for six copies, while the total order for Leinster was one hundred and fifty-seven copies.[33]

As query number thirty-five indicated, care was to be taken that apprentices and servants be placed among Friends (the preference was that Quakers would be employed by Quakers). Permission was required from meetings to take on apprentices of another denomination. Numerous entries in the minutes of Moate men's monthly meeting mention those who took up apprenticeships and some entries named the master (a small number from the Ballymurray meeting) to whom they would be indentured. Other entries mentioned the trade to be undertaken, such as tanning, linen-weaving, bridle-cutting, tailoring, felt-making and shoe-making. Two boys, the children of Ann Hogg, in want of maintenance, clothing and education were attended to by Moate meeting from early 1765 until late 1772. Clothing, accommodation, books and school fees were paid for a Joseph Hogg on a quarterly basis.[34] William Hogg, brother of Joseph, was apprenticed to James McGaw, a linen weaver of Killarney (townland), for the term of seven years. In March 1765, with the aid of the provincial meeting, his widowed mother was supported with £4 towards William's clothing and apprentice fee.[35]

Unlike John Tennant, a well-behaved apprentice examined by Leanne Calvert, William Hogg was disowned in September 1772. The cause was 'that he had absconded some time ago from his master

James McGaw and left a young woman of the neighbourhood with child'; William served five years of his seven-year apprenticeship.[36] The master James McGaw and his wife Prudence née Fairbrother enrolled their fourteen-year-old son John in the Leinster provincial school of Mountmellick for the year 1788–9. In 1797–8 Elizabeth McLean, daughter of James and Susanna, was enrolled by her grandfather Nathan Nevitt. James McLean, Nathan Nevitt's son-in-law, had served his apprenticeship in Nathan's linen business. A consequence of Quaker commitment to egalitarianism was that many Quaker apprentices could aspire to marry their master's daughters, thus expanding the Quaker network.[37] These are the only two enrolments from Ballymurray for Mountmellick provincial school up to 1789, and this suggests that, as linen-weavers, both the McGaws and McLeans could afford at this time to pay for some education for at least one of their children. A further twenty-four children either from or connected to Ballymurray attended the provincial school between the years 1790 and 1852, about half of whose education was supported financially by the Moate meeting.[38]

By the late 1750s Ballymurray Quakers had lost some of their original members, due to disownments, infirmity and death. By this point the linen industry of Ballymurray area was in decline, as demonstrated by the migration of John Nevitt to America for work. This decline in the linen industry and the need to migrate for work was not isolated to Ballymurray and was experienced throughout Ireland.[39] The Ballymurray community continued to experience challenges, especially as the early arrivals aged. James Burne of Galey, one of the first Ballymurray Quakers, was described in early 1749 'as a most steady and exemplary member who was much impaired of health and memory to absent himself from attending meetings'.[40] Thomas Siggins, who had arrived at Ballymurray with James Burne, was disowned from the Society of Friends in 1750 because 'he do not condemn the behaviour of his daughters', Anne and Margaret. Margaret was accused 'of marrying out of the Quakers and keeping in company of her sister' Anne and her husband Benjamin Knott, who ran a 'tippling house'; both actions were considered scandalous.[41] The loss of these two elderly members marked the beginning of a period of significant decline in Ballymurray Quaker membership.[42] Certificates for removal from Moate were granted in early 1748 for six of the Ballymurray Quakers. Two of these, Nathan Nevitt and his wife Mary, returned to Ballymurray in March 1750. Certificates for removal to Pennsylvania were also sought and granted between 1750 and 1755 for four men from Ballymurray.[43] Among those that left for America were Nathan Nevitt's brothers, John and William. John stated that he went for employment, but he returned to Ballymurray after one year. Seven disownments due to marrying out of the Quaker community occurred between 1745 and 1759. Six other disownments were recorded during the period 1740–50 caused by running up debts and failing to settle with creditors. On 15 September 1753 Edward Alexander moved from Galey to Limerick with a certificate approved by Moate. He had served his apprenticeship in the tailor trade of Moate.[44] An Elizabeth Gibbs née Cantrell, wife of Nicholas who was disowned for insolvency, was reported to have 'joined with the Methodists' and consequently was disowned in 1749.[45] While canvassing in Aughrim, Co. Galway, in 1748, the Methodist leader John Wesley was said to have baptized seven Quakers from Roscommon.[46] Elizabeth is the only Quaker of Leinster province in 1749 to have converted to Methodism, at least as recorded in the minutes of 1749. In total the Ballymurray community reduced by thirty people, either in a permanent or in a temporary capacity. This must have had a demoralizing effect on this already small community. The challenges for such a small community were clearly multi-faceted: advancing age and infirmity, migration, finances, unemployment, the attraction of other religious groups and scarcity of suitable marriage partners.

It is telling that in 1755 members of Moate meeting decided to visit Ballymurray on a more frequent basis to offer assistance and guidance.[47] It also appears that for a short period a meeting was held in Athlone (probably in the home of William Sproule), which was also visited by Moate members; in total seven visits were carried out between September 1755 and September 1757.[48]

That the Ballymurray Quaker community was under some pressure was already evident from an account to the Moate monthly meeting in April 1750 that recorded 'a very unsatisfactory meeting in Ballymurray'. Despite advice frequently given, the Ballymurray members 'appeared cold and indifferent to religion'.[49] Eventually, in December 1757 Moate decided to end weekday meetings in

Ballymurray, reducing pressure on the depleted community there. Losing so many members underlined the many difficulties faced by the community, as indeed did the successful movement of Quakers from Ballymurray to other locations, such as Edward Alexander's move to Limerick in 1753, which provided many viable opportunities for trade and commerce.[50] It appears that in the 1740s and 1750s location mattered.

The legal case for title to Mote Park and the Crofton estate was described by Marcus Lowther Crofton in 1751 as 'a long and vexatious lawsuit of six years and two months'.[51] The legacy of this case was financial uncertainty for Mote Park estate, which was not resolved until 1776. It was arranged for Marcus's son Edward to lease Mote for £500 per annum while the remainder of the estate allowed Marcus £1,000 per annum. The rest of his income was to be used to pay his debts. The lease and conveyance for this arrangement was executed in late 1776. The following December, Charles Frizell produced a survey map of Mote Park estate and several surrounding townlands.[52] For over twenty years debts from the lawsuit shadowed Mote Park and the estate, but revival and renewed growth was made possible with Edward's leasing of the estate. According to *The Crofton memoirs*, Mote Park house was constructed in 1778, and this must have generated employment with a sense of progress and renewed possibility.[53]

A similar pattern was evident in Ballymurray Quaker community, the result of support provided by Moate men's meeting. In August 1773 several Moate members agreed to a new lease with Sir Marcus Lowther Crofton for Ballymurray meeting house and burial ground. This was to be completed as hastily as possible because the existing lease was for the term of one life. This measure alone confirms a commitment to the future of Ballymurray meeting on the part of Moate meeting, although it may also have presented an opportunity to take advantage of the difficulties of Mote Park estate and its owner. The measures taken by the Moate meeting in 1757 to aid Ballymurray had proved disappointing. In fact, in 1778 Moate Quakers chastised Ballymurray members for their neglect and non-attendance. By this stage, the Moate meeting was offering consistent support; between 1775 and 1785, the Moate monthly meeting took place in Ballymurray meeting house once a year.

Ballymurray needed to retain membership and, indeed, to increase its numbers, which explains why the community was willing to adapt the rules and to sanction readmission of former members after a transgression had been denounced. Without readmission of contrite members, the Ballymurray Quaker community would have declined earlier. The Robinson family of Killarney demonstrated a fluctuating commitment to the Quaker community that lasted through four generations of continual adaptation. In the census of Elphin, Jonathan Robinson of Killarney was denoted as 'Protestant' and he had been recently disowned by the Society of Friends for marrying a person of another denomination (on the death of his first wife Hannah Boate, he married a Catholic). Jonathan's son, Thomas, was disowned in April 1770 for the attempted abduction of Elizabeth Nevitt. Thomas's written apology of September 1773 was accepted, as we have seen, and he married Elizabeth Alexander in Ballymurray meeting house on 12 November 1773. Thomas and his wife had nine children between 1775 and 1791, six of whom where disowned for 'marrying out'. Their grandchild, Charles Robinson, had a request for membership made on his behalf by his mother, Hannah Robinson, wife of George, in 1814.[54]

Sir Edward Crofton initiated a renewed drive for the improvement of Mote Park estate on his succession to the baronetcy and estate, in 1784. He placed an advertisement in *Faulkner's Dublin Journal* in January 1784, which sought Protestant workmen and a manufacturing business to settle in Ballymurray. The advertisement promoted the linen or woollen industries, the advantages of the location and access to the Shannon. It also stated that a stipulated sum of money would be provided on completion of houses built to an approved plan.[55] The article mentioned that an old mill would be removed, although an exact location of the development was not provided. On the 1777 Frizell survey of the Crofton estate a reference page and map titled 'Corgorrow' details another survey by a Mr Burke and thirteen acres named Newfoundland. This may have been the land on which the cottages for the 1784 advert were to be situated. The article of 1784 suggests there was a failing or defunct linen or yarn industry in the area. Isaac Weld's 1832 *Statistical survey of County Roscommon* informed the reader that the desertion of a little district of neat cottages and excellent hedges and enclosures, formerly inhabited by Quaker linen workers, was caused by the decline in the linen and yarn industry.[56] From both of these sources it is evident that linen workers were employed in this locality; that they were Quakers is understood from both Weld's *Survey* and Quaker records. The constantly changing conditions of the Crofton landlords and the linen market required adaptation to the environment and employment opportunities. It is probable that the evolution of the linen and yarn industry of Ballymurray had several stages of decline and progress, but very few memorials to the industry remain.[57]

The Ballymurray community encouraged the admission of new members and in two cases it appears to have been by reason of marriage. Jonathan Beale applied for membership in 1785 shortly before marrying Anne Burne, daughter of John Burne of Galey, in January 1786. Jonathan's membership was short lived for he was disowned in June 1790 for failing to satisfy the demands of his creditors and because 'Jonathan Beale avoids Friends; business is beyond his abilities'.[58] Vincent Pellet arrived from Eyrecourt, Co. Galway, and applied for membership in July 1786. He married Mary Burne, daughter of John Burne of Galey, in Moate meeting house on 10 January 1787. Vincent Pellet remained in Ballymurray after his wife Mary passed away and married, secondly, Rachel Jessop from Edenderry meeting on 16 October 1808.[59] Rachel and Vincent were dedicated Quaker members with many mentions in the minutes of Moate men's monthly meeting. No births were recorded for the Pellet marriages and, although loyal Quakers of Ballymurray, they do not appear to have helped in increasing their numbers.

Attempts were also made to lure lapsed members back to Ballymurray meeting. Members of the Moate community visited William Sproule of Athlone and John Burne of Rockhill, Carrownolan, near Athlone, to ask about their and their families' absence from Ballymurray meetings in the years 1784–6. In September 1784 William Sproule, his wife Elizabeth and family were called to answer for their lack of attendance. William's age and state of health were the reasons given to Moate members. After William's death and the difficulties with the execution of a will between Joseph Sproule and his sister, attempts were made by the Moate members to convince William's children to re-join the Moate meeting. William junior agreed 'to walk with Friends', but his sister, Sarah Sproule, 'did not desire to be considered a member', a decision recorded in the minutes of Moate men's meeting in May 1789. Sarah Sproule must have accepted membership for a short period, for she was disowned by Moate meeting in July 1804 for 'marrying out'.[60] John Burne of Carrownolan was visited by Friends from Moate meeting, and advised on several occasions regarding the absence of himself and his children between December 1785 and February 1786.[61] Several newspapers stated that John Burne of Rockhill was murdered on 25 September 1826 and it appears that the Quakers remembered him as a member of the Society of Friends.[62] It is probable that the Burnes of Carrownolan and the Sproules of Athlone were wealthy, lapsed members of the Ballymurray community. Their children were encouraged to re-join, which indicates a relaxation of rules, fewer disownments of absentees and a renewed need to attract new members, particularly those familiar with Quakerism.

The case of James McLean who married Susanna Nevitt (Nathan's daughter) in 1773 demonstrates an increasing flexibility in the application of the rules, presumably in an attempt to retain prominent members. James had attended the national half-yearly meeting in Dublin in November 1773 and May 1774, as a member of Leinster Province.[63] From James's marriage in 1773 until late 1775, Moate men's meeting repeatedly made inquiries 'to seek the true actions' regarding James and his creditors. Newspaper reports from June 1774 noted that James McLean was robbed of £182 on 17 May with which he was to buy yarn the next day. The robbers were said to have broken into his house and held a knife to his throat.[64] During the inquiry into this affair, Ballymurray Quakers were noted for their absence from several meetings, which delayed proceedings. McLean was eventually disowned in July 1775. The testimony against him stated that he had falsified his financial status to his in-laws and was unable to pay his creditors.[65]

During the years between 1740 and 1788 the Ballymurray Quakers struggled to respond to a series of challenges. Their membership stagnated as a result of the many disownments, which were greater than the level of births and new admissions. Quakers were seen (by themselves and self-promoted as such) as honest people who traded with fairness and principle, and this was important as they relied upon this perceived honesty for economic reasons. To ensure that

Quaker numbers remained sustainable and undiluted, it was also important for Quakers to marry Quakers. The harm to the reputation of the Friends resulting from transgressions was the most commonly mentioned feature of disownments and arbitration cases. None of the years covered by this chapter appear to have been easy, but the micro-community of Ballymurray Quakers 'hung on by a thread', many of them clinging to their meeting house and membership with dogged tenacity. The range of sources examined indicates that the community settled into the wider locality, supporting and having a vested interest in the affairs of the Crofton landlords. They maintained their unique identity through education, trade and worship, while forgiving some members who failed to adhere to the Quaker rules.

3. The decline of the Ballymurray Quaker community, 1789–1848

This chapter discusses the Ballymurray Quaker community in the final period of its existence. A number of events impacted on it in the late eighteenth and early nineteenth centuries, notably the deaths of three lords Crofton, proprietors of Mote Park, in 1784, 1797 and 1816. Sir Edward Crofton was 11 years old when he succeeded to the baronetcy 'of the Mote in its second creation'.[1] As a result, he did not take up residence on the estate for fifteen years. As we have already seen, the fortunes of the Quakers were closely intertwined with those of the Croftons, and the long absence impacted negatively on them. Among the Quakers themselves, it is probable that only the Burnes of Galey had enough wealth to buffer themselves against adversity.

Minutes of Moate men's meeting are available for most of this period, and they point to a continual decline of the Quakers of Ballymurray between 1789 and 1848. In addition to difficulties experienced by the Croftons, the chapter shows that the decline was the result of several factors, which included an ageing Quaker population in Ballymurray, very few new members, financial difficulties and a change of attitude by some of the most respected members of the community to the acquisition and use of arms. The tensions preceding the 1798 rebellion (particularly from 1793) and the aftereffects (up to 1810) impacted on the Ballymurray community and were reflected in tithes, parish cess and goods distrained for military purposes.

Ballymurray meeting is mentioned throughout the entire set of Moate minutes for this period, but the individuals of Ballymurray are very infrequently noted from 1817. The records of Ballymurray and its community fade softly into almost total silence around 1822. There is a very telling account of the state of the Ballymurray and Moate meetings in an 1818 report to the provincial meeting held in Carlow. Ballymurray, at that stage, claimed a membership of twenty individuals, with ten to twelve of those attending first-day meetings, and only five to six attending the fifth-day meeting.[2] The sources permit the reconstruction of the little community at that point, including age profile, as well as marital and employment status. The very small, ageing Quaker community of Ballymurray met with several challenges during this period, which they might have survived if they had had the support of a 'stronger' Moate meeting, a resident and affluent landlord, youth, wealth and a commitment to Quaker beliefs above personal survival.

The events of the 1790s, in particular the Rebellion of 1798, were felt in all Irish Quaker communities, where individuals were encouraged to remain neutral as befitting a society of pacifists.[3] Roscommon remained remote to most of the events of 1798, but the minutes of national meetings reflected an awareness of the concerns of Quakers across the island. At the April 1796 national meeting members voiced concern regarding the possession of arms and indicated that all members should surrender their weapons.[4]

The results were reported in the minutes of many Quaker meetings throughout the country. In April 1796 it was reported at the Moate monthly meeting that 'Friends continue to keep arms in their houses, which may be used for destruction of mankind'. The minutes suggested that a reliance on divine protection rather than arms was more in keeping with their religious practices.[5] The minutes also recorded several calls for the surrender of arms and provided details of those who were reluctant to relinquish the weapons in their possession. A Moate report dated May 1797 listed seven individuals who refrained from giving up their arms.[6] Nathan Nevitt of Ballymurray had to explain why a member of his family held a firearm. He stated that the 'person was no longer a member of the society' and declared that 'the firearm would not be kept on their property'.[7] In February 1797 Lawford Burne was disowned for joining 'those armed associations lately established', possibly a reference to the yeomanry created in 1796.[8] Burne would later join the army, but 1797 was the first sign of his move away from Quaker pacifism.[9] He and his brother Godfrey, who moved to Dublin, had certificates issued in 1793 that placed them into 'the care of the Dublin Friends'. There are no Quaker birth records for either Lawford or Godfrey (they were either cousins or nephews of John Burne of Rockhill), but

The decline of the Ballymurray Quaker community, 1789–1848

Table 1. Twenty Ballymurray Quakers in 1818

Name	Marital status	Age in 1818 (years)	Residence	Death
Lewis, John	Married in 1830	30	Racecourse, Moneymore	1841
Lewis, John	Married to Abigail	62	Racecourse, Moneymore	1818
Lewis, Abigail	Married to John	56	Racecourse, Moneymore	1837
Lewis, George	Single	18	Racecourse, Moneymore	1819
Pellet, Vincent	Married in 1808	64	Ballymurray	1837
Pellet, Rachel	Married in 1808	51	Ballymurray	1846
Fairbrother, Edward	Widower	53	Portrunny & Quaker Island	1838
Fairbrother, Hannah	Married in 1834	17	Portrunny & Quaker Island	1840
Wigglesworth, William	Single	26	Ballymurray/Dublin	1822
Wigglesworth, Joseph	Single	c.24	Ballymurray/Mountmellick	?
Burne, Sarah	Single	17	Ballymurray	?
Burne, Joseph/James	Single	14	Ballymurray, Rockhill	1828
Burne, John	Single	19	Ballymurray	?
Barton, Elizabeth (Nevitt)	Widow	68	Ballymurray	1819
Alexander, Rachell (Nevitt)	Widow	60	Racepark, Moneymore	1847
Alexander, Mary (Nevitt)	Widow	65	Newtown, Curry	1822
Alexander, John	Single	24	Newtown, Curry	?
Alexander, Jane	Married in 1830	27	Newtown, Curry	1858
Burne, John	Single?	c.60	Rockhill, Carrownolan	1826
Beale, Anne (Burne)	Widow	62	Churchpark, Athleague	1833

(sources: FHLD MSS H.1, H.2, H.3, H.6, H.12, H.18, H.19, H.4E)

the 1793 certificates suggest they applied for membership as children of disowned Quaker parents. The significance of the cases of Nathan Nevitt and Lawford Burne is that they were both important members of the small Quaker community in Ballymurray. The Nevitts were an active Quaker family, and the Burnes were wealthy Quakers, descendants of James Burne of Galey. Both of these influential families showed signs of dissent from the pacifism of the Society of Friends. Considering that, at most, just eight Quaker families were resident in the Ballymurray compass, this must have had a rather unsettling effect on the community.

For the Ballymurray Quakers, the 1790s marked a time of major change in both membership numbers and the family circumstances of those who remained. One important change was the decision in May 1797 to discontinue the winter half-yearly national meeting and to hold a yearly national meeting, which commenced on the last first-day of April 1798, in Dublin.[10] This decision would reduce the need for Friends to journey to Dublin on a biannual basis and it probably reduced the network and kinship engendered by Quaker meetings. National meetings were held in Dublin over a four-to-five-day period and were a social gathering for Quakers, a place to meet friends and family, and to exchange news and ideas; they also provided opportunities to arrange marriage partnerships.[11]

During the final decade of the eighteenth century, five people sought membership of the Ballymurray Quakers; at the same time, over fifteen members were disowned. Membership levels could not be maintained in those circumstances. One of those who sought admittance was Robert Wigglesworth of Ballymurray. He was husband to Sarah Burne who had been disowned for this marriage, but she was readmitted in 1798 after providing a written apology.[12] Robert became a valued member of the Ballymurray meeting and was noted for his service to the community, including the negotiation of a lease renewal for Ballymurray meeting house and burial ground in 1803–4.

At a meeting of Quakers held in Moate on 8 September 1802 it was reported that the lease for Ballymurray meeting house and burial ground had expired. Those assembled chose Robert Wigglesworth and Anthony Robinson (of Moate and lease-holder of 274 acres in Galey) to seek a new lease with the landowner 'as a matter of urgency'.[13] The lease renewal for Ballymurray was discussed at Moate men's monthly meeting in April, July and September 1803. On 6 April 1804 the meeting noted that a lease had been agreed by the proprietor, Edward Crofton, for three lives or thirty-one years, with the stipulation that the premises be first 'decently repaired'.[14] Wigglesworth and John Russell (of Moate) supervised the lease renewal and repairs to Ballymurray meeting house. On 19 September 1804 Moate men's monthly meeting recorded that subscriptions of £29 8s. 6d. had been raised for repairs to Ballymurray meeting house, and the treasurer was requested to pay Thomas Robinson the sum of £4 6s. 12d. to make up the sum of thirty guineas, previously agreed to be remitted by the meeting. The previous month's report stated that the repair works were almost complete, but that the cost would exceed £50; the amount raised by Ballymurray Friends was £24 15s. 9d.[15] The 1804 lease for Ballymurray meeting house and burial grounds was discussed at a meeting in Moate in 1813, probably to examine details after the death of Wigglesworth.[16] In renewing the lease, the Moate and Ballymurray Quaker communities expressed their commitment to their continuance in the locality, and this was reinforced by the expense and maintenance expended on the premises. In contrast to this was the social and economic unrest that had developed in the previous two decades. The Ballymurray Quakers were optimistic for their survival for the next few decades, but their records illustrate that this hope was misplaced. Ballymurray Quaker numbers were declining and this must have impacted their standing within their locality and the community at large.

The optimism of the Ballymurray Quakers relating to their survival was reflected in a report of December 1817 on the state of their meeting. While no members of Moate meeting attended the provincial meeting in Carlow on 29 December 1817, in response to a request for information they submitted a detailed report on the state of the Moate and Ballymurray meetings, covering membership, attendance, the nature of meetings and their frequency.[17] This report was read twice at the meeting in Moate on 10 December 1817 and, once agreed, it was signed and given to John Russell of Moate to send to the quarterly provincial meeting.[18] The provincial meeting recorded scant details regarding the reports on Moate or Ballymurray, but the entire report was transcribed in the minutes of Moate men's meeting on 10 December 1817. At this point, Moate had a membership of 120 individuals with 'better than half actively attending'. In comparison, Ballymurray had a mere twenty individual members, with ten to twelve attending first-day mornings (they did not hold afternoon meetings), and five to six attending fifth-day meetings.[19] The low numbers explain, in part, why there was a lack of entries for Ballymurray individuals in Quaker records of the period and especially in Moate minutes after 1818. They could no longer have been considered to constitute a viable community. A short description of the twenty Ballymurray Quaker individuals has been compiled and includes their marital status and age (table 1).

The twenty individuals of the December 1817 report included three Nevitt sisters, who had all married and were by then widowed. Just two married couples lived within the Ballymurray area. The first couple was Vincent and Rachel Pellet, who lived in Ballymurray townland and do not appear to have had children. Vincent Pellet is accounted for in the tithe applotment books for Ballymurray in 1827 when he was farming ten acres of second-quality land and three acres, three roods of third-quality land in Killea.[20] John and Abigail Lewis of Racecourse (an area within the townland of Moneymore) were the second married couple. John Lewis farmed nineteen acres of second-quality land at 8*d*. per acre in Moneymore in 1827.[21] John and Abigail had two sons, George born in 1800 and John born in 1788. Within eighteen months of the report John Lewis senior and his son George had died.[22] Jane Alexander, aged 27, resided in the townland of Newtown and married John Lewis (son of John and Abigail) on 19 August 1830.[23]

The remaining ten individuals recorded in the 1817 report included three Burne teenagers: John, Joseph and Sarah, children of the late John Burne, who all attended the provincial school at Mountmellick and were in immediate need of permanent apprenticeship placements.[24] John was apprenticed on a trial basis to a William and Richard Neale of Coolrain, Co. Laois.[25] Sarah's certificate of placement in Mountmellick meeting was prepared in March 1817. Joseph was harder to place because he had declined going to a place of apprentice even after the provincial meeting secured the necessary fee.[26] Finally, Joseph was recorded as bound as apprentice to a linen weaver in the compass of Richhill, Co. Armagh, in April 1821. For a period of five years, his master was to clothe him, and a fee of £10 was agreed to be managed by John Russell of Moate.[27] Robert and Sarah Wigglesworth had died by 1807 and their sons William, 26 years old, and Joseph, his younger brother, moved frequently before settling. William moved between Dublin and Ballymurray, while Joseph moved between Mountmellick and Ballymurray. In the tithe applotment books for 1834 for 'Turmane', probably Tromaun (which is just south-west of Mote Park), one Joseph Wigglesworth farmed forty-seven of the 178 acres.[28] The remaining individuals included a widow, Anne Beale of Churchpark, Athleague. Widow Beale had received financial assistance of 5s. per week from Moate meeting from 1813 to 1814. Her son Samuel, who had died in May 1812, had required assistance from Moate meeting. In December 1811 it recorded 'from indisposition rendered incapable to maintain himself, and needs assistance, Vincent Pellet is provided with £5 for his care' (his funeral costs were also covered by Moate meeting).[29] The final members noted in the report were Edward Fairbrother, a widower, and his daughter Hannah, of Ballymurray, with land in Portrunny and Quaker Island, who were both active members of Ballymurray meeting. Hannah later married William Odlum of Roscommon in the last Quaker marriage to take place in Ballymurray meeting house on 18 December 1834.[30] The second last member of the 'Ballymurray twenty' may have been John Burne of Rockhill, who had earlier been admonished for poor attendance. He was registered in the book of Moate deaths of 1826. The final member was John Alexander who was disowned in August 1818 for marrying in a manner contrary to the rules of the society.[31]

The 1817 report depicted a very small community with half of the members over the age of 50 years, many of them widowed. It is also evident from an examination of the Moate minutes that several Ballymurray Quakers required financial assistance. The small community faced an inevitable disintegration due to the death of its aged members, the departure of younger members and few if any replacements in the form of new members. It is probable that none of the twenty individuals of Ballymurray in late 1817 were of the 'strong-farmer' status; they were for the most part elderly, widowed or unmarried and in need of employment.

The small community of Ballymurray Quakers realized the precariousness of their situation, as expressed in the report: 'Onto the state of our meeting, it is certainly low for various painfully distressing circumstances have affected this monthly meeting'. The report went on to infer that without the assistance of the quarterly meeting, they would have no cause for hope.[32] A spirit of their perseverance is evident in a note dated May 1833, which was added to the family page of George Russell and his wife, Margaret née Wyly of Thomastown, in the minutes of Moate men's monthly meeting.[33] This recorded: 'There are seventy members including the Ballymurray Friends belonging to the monthly meeting of Moate Granoge, what a small membership yet if these keep their places in the Truth, these may yet be a fulfilment of the prophecy – A little one shall become a thousand and a small one strong nation I the Lord will hasten in this time'.[34] It is noteworthy that in the sixteen years between 1817 and 1833 the combined membership of Moate and Ballymurray meetings reduced from 140 to seventy members, marking a very rapid decline in the pre-Famine decades noted for a general population increase. For the Ballymurray Quakers, it was significant that January 1816 marked the beginning of seventeen years of Crofton absence from the locality on the death of Sir Edward Crofton, 3rd baronet in its second creation. His son and heir, another Edward, grew up in England and did not return to reside at Mote Park until his marriage in 1833. This would have added to a sense of neglect and abandonment of the area.[35] Weld's *Statistical survey of the county of Roscommon* reflected this feeling of abandonment: 'Mote Park was not only uninhabited, but devoid of furniture when I saw it, and had a most melancholy appearance'.[36]

In the decade following the report of December 1817 one can track the continued decline of the Ballymurray Quaker community. For the years 1818–28 it is possible to document Quaker individuals who had goods taken from them in lieu of tithes (which the Quakers referred to as sufferings) and compare that information with the tithe applotment books and the 1828 Cooke survey of the Crofton estate.[37] Moate minutes of this period mention several cases of insolvency and bankruptcy and one of speculation, some of which explain changes in landholdings among the Quakers of Ballymurray. Speculation and insolvency were experienced in 1813–15 by some of the Robinson family who held land in Galey, and this had a negative impact on the financial status of Ballymurray Quakers. Landholdings of this period in what were or had been Quaker family names have been identified through the Moate records of sufferings for the period 1788–1859 and the tithe applotment books (table 2).

The decline of the Ballymurray Quaker community, 1789–1848

Table 2. Ballymurray area with Quaker and former Quaker holdings, 1827

Civil parish	Townland	Tithe payer	Area	Value
Kilmeane	Ballymurray	Vincent Pellet (Quaker)	10a.	6s. 8d.
Kilmeane	Ballymurray	John Jackson	9a.	6s.
Kilmeane	Boggin/Bogganfin	Samuel Jackson	72a.	£2 8s.
Kilmeane	Curgorrow/Corgarve	Mr George Fairbrother	9a.	4s. 8d.
Kilmeane	Curry	Col. Trench T. Robinson	151a. 3r.	£5 16s. 8d.
Kilmeane	Moneymore	William Siggins	11a. 2r. 30p.	7s. 10d.
Kilmeane	Moneymore	John Lewis (Quaker)	19a.	12s. 8d.
Kilmeane	Portrunny	Mr George Fairbrother	20a.	£3
Kilmeane	Portrunny	George Siggins	16a.	£1
Killinvoy	Ballygalda/Stonepark	Edward Fairbrother	19a.	16s. 3d.
Killinvoy	Galey	Thomas Robinson	124a. 2r.	£5 13s. 6d.
Killinvoy	Galey	Lawford Burne	86a.	£3 17s.
Killinvoy	Galey	Edward Burne	52a. 2r.	£2 7s. 5d.
Killinvoy	Galey	William Robinson	274a.	£11 7s. 8d.
Killinvoy	Shragh/Srah	John Alexander	25a. 1r.	4s.
Roscommon	Ballymartin Beg	Anthony Wigglesworth	20a. 1r. 3p.	16s. 8d.
Roscommon	Ballymartin Beg	Joseph Wigglesworth	7a. 1r. 3p.	5s. 10d.

(source: Tithe applotment books, National Archives of Ireland. a. = acres; r. = roods; p. = perches)

Moate book of sufferings for 1788–1859 recorded those from whom tithes had been taken each year. In the document the Ballymurray Quakers were recorded as Co. Roscommon inhabitants. Each individual record detailed the landholder. This sometimes included a distinguishing word, for example Thomas Robinson Killarney, was differentiated from Thomas Robinson Moate, also Thomas 'Anty' Robinson. The individual records included the names of the tithe takers, their assistants, the tithe mongers, the priest and parish to which the tithe was due. They also included the distribution of the tithe due, the names of the second set of collectors and to whom the second proportion was due. Indeed, the documentation provides an impressive range of information concerning land-use, crops grown and their value, change of landholder, civil parish names and variations, priests' names, landlords' names and the names of those employed to collect the tithes. Significantly, the list of sufferings for this period varied in several ways from the earlier set of sufferings, available for 1719–23.[38] Obvious differences were the changes of landholder names, names of priests and tithe-takers. The unexpected information garnered was evidence of cyclical change in land-use, crops grown, their value and especially the tithes taken (amounting to 42 sheep in total) for military purposes between 1803 and 1810. The records illustrate the changing circumstances of landholders: some of them held multiple scattered holdings, and graziers and tillage farmers are identifiable from this set of records. Flax was taken as tithes from several of the Quakers of Ballymurray and this points to a long association with both the farms, farmers and weavers of the area, confirming a connection to the linen industry of Co. Roscommon. The last flax taken as tithes was from John Gaw in 1794. This was another indicator of the changing circumstances that faced the Quakers of Ballymurray, following the depressions in the Irish linen industry in the 1750s and 1760s.[39]

The difficulties experienced by the Robinson family further affected the Ballymurray Quakers. On 13 April 1814 Moate meeting was informed that Anthony, son of Anthony Robinson, had become insolvent. In May 1815 George Robinson was listed as bankrupt, and in July 1815 the meeting recorded that Samuel Robinson had 'speculated to proceed with unwarrantable extension of trade, beyond his own capital to support and, having large properties of others to hand, acknowledges he was tempted, which has fatally terminated to the loss of those whose properties were committed'.[40] Moate meeting recorded similar accounts over the next two years of other insolvencies, which also reinforce the view that Quakers who lived in Ballymurray held an average of ten to twelve acres, while those who leased larger farms of land in this area, particularly at Galey, held or managed multiple farms in different areas. Anthony Robinson resided in Moate, while George Robinson in 1812 had parish cess taken from him for three counties: Roscommon, Westmeath and Queen's County (now Laois).[41] Adherence to Quaker rules was difficult and led to some reduction in Quaker members. Indeed, evidence suggests that former Quakers continued to work land in Ballymurray, just not as members of the Society of Friends. This is evident from comparison of landholding in Ballymurray in 1777 and 1828. The Frizell survey of Mote Park, carried out in 1777, contained the names of twelve Quaker tenants and included Alexander, Burne, Jackson, Nevitt and Robinson with a total of 978a. 3r. 32p. under lease.[42] The tenant with the least land (1a. 2r. 24p.) was Nathan Nevitt of Ballymurray who was noted as having no lease; the largest landholder was Anthony Robinson who leased 280a. 3r. 22p. at Galey. In 1828, the tithe applotment books recorded that 924 acres were associated with contemporary or former Ballymurray Quaker family names.

The two sources – of 1777 and 1828 – record a similar acreage held by the same families, either by marriage or birth, but it is also evident that they did not all remain in Quaker membership. This suggests that the Ballymurray locality provided sustainable livelihoods for those who farmed the 924 acres between 1777 and 1828. The 1828 Cooke survey and maps of the estate of Lord Crofton are held in Roscommon County Library and provide an important snapshot of landholding in the area.[43] The survey has detailed lists of tenants and their holdings in the townlands connected with Quakers. By 1828, only three Quaker family names are listed: George Fairbrother of Corgarve with just over nine acres; John Jackson (named as a tithe-taker in Quaker records) of Ballymurray with over six acres; and John Alexander of the area called Srah, which is north of Knockcroghery townland. The source does not indicate an acreage for Alexander as he seemed to own this land himself.[44] The last entries for Ballymurray Quakers in their records of sufferings were added in 1827 and 1832. The book of sufferings for Roscommon notes only one person in 1827, William Robinson who had tithes due to the value of £5 13s. 6d. The tithe-collectors took four sheep from him valued at £4 15s. One further entry was made for Roscommon in 1832, when Revd Peter Brown of Kilmeane civil parish demanded £2 4s. 8d. from John Lewis; one heifer was taken from his farm valued at £2 15s.[45] John Lewis had married Jane Alexander on 19 August 1830 and they resided at Racecourse near Moneymore. As the Quakers fell away, aged or were disowned, they did not necessarily leave the locality. Individual family names associated with the Quaker community of Ballymurray remained long after the discontinuance of the meeting itself in 1848. The minutes of Moate men's meeting appear to be lost for the years

1822–43, so other sources have been considered, including records produced by Quaker visitors to the region.

Accounts written by visitors to the area generally depicted an unruly native population, and those prepared by three Quaker visitors, Jesse Kersey in 1804, and Elizabeth Fry and her brother Joseph John Gurney in 1827, upheld this view, although to differing degrees. Visits by Quakers who were called into ministry were recorded in the minutes of many meetings and several eminent Quakers visited Ballymurray. The American Quaker Jesse Kersey visited Ballymurray in 1804 and recorded a very negative portrayal of the native Irish:

> Attended a small meeting at this place, which is the only meeting of Friends in the Province of Connacht. The members, few in number, and it appears as though for some time to come to this quarter must be given up to its superstitious inhabitants. Indeed, I have often had serious doubts whether it may not be a length of time before much good can be expected in many parts of this nation. The degraded situation of many of its inhabitants appears to me so vast that nothing but a vigorous effort of suffering humanity or a bold and venturous propagation of truth will ever be sufficient to raise objects of wretchedness to their proper rank in the society of mankind.[46]

Elizabeth Fry was a prominent prison reformer who visited women prisoners throughout Ireland along with her brother in 1827. She and Joseph John Gurney attended meetings throughout their tour. On 24 March 1827 they attended one at Ballymurray.[47] Elizabeth and Joseph kept journals, which included accounts of their 1827 visit. Elizabeth's journal was edited by two of her daughters and published in 1847; Joseph's was published in 1855.[48] Both journals mentioned their presence at a meeting in Ballymurray which was well attended by the small group of Friends of Ballymurray. Elizabeth reflected positively on the efforts made by the Friends to attend such meetings for she had been advised that the road had been vandalized (this proved false but attested to the tensions of the period). In Ballymurray they lodged in the clean comfortable farmhouse of a widow, Margaret Robinson, and her interesting family of young people. Elizabeth had no fire in her room but was struck by the kindness of the Friends;

she admired 'their efforts through true religion, in changing the nature of this people, making them clean, courteous and gentle'. Both Elizabeth and Joseph remarked on the murderers held in Roscommon and Mullingar prisons, and Joseph detailed the ten prisoners held in Roscommon for the murder of a member of the Society of Friends, a nominal Friend (John Burne of Rockhill near Athlone), who held a quantity of arms at his house.[49]

The murder of John Burne of Rockhill (the house name and an electoral division – the Burne residence was in Carrownolan townland) was widely reported in local, national and English newspapers. The reports differed slightly but they provide an illustration of the tensions in Co. Roscommon in the 1820s. In most articles Burne was described as a 'Quaker Gentleman of considerable wealth and skills of husbandry'.[50] In the 27 September 1826 edition of the *Morning Post,* Burne was described as follows: 'he was one of the Society of Quakers but declined in late years in attending their meetings and showed no signs of the clothing usually worn by that society'. The article also intimated that his murder may have been perpetrated by the temptation of Burne's considerable fortune.[51] Directly after this article, the newspaper published what they titled 'Another account', which detailed the robbery at Burne's house and his murder – this story was carried by several Irish and English newspapers around the same time.[52] One particular newspaper article in the *Caledonian Mercury* expanded on the detail of the robbery and stated 'that three stand of firearms' had been taken from Burne's house.[53]

Immediately after the murder, notice of a reward for the apprehension and conviction of the perpetrators was published in a number of newspapers. The notice included the names of up to twenty gentlemen and the amounts they contributed to the reward. At the head of this list was one Lawford Burne.[54] On 4 October 1826 the chief constable, T.S. Ireland, reported to Major Warburton that the police had apprehended nine individuals near Athlone who were suspects in the murder.[55] Between December 1828 and January 1829, extracts of the same letter appeared in several newspapers, in which it was stated that Ballymurray had received its first visit from the Rockites.[56] Several Protestant families, who had their windows and furniture smashed and broken, were also beaten, by the 200–300 'lads' or Rockites who had gathered that night.[57] The letter stated that on

20 December the Roscommon police had come across two men in Killarney townland in possession of two pistols, a powder horn, two flints, a prayer book and two Rockite notices.[58]

In June 1831 an article published in the *Freeman's Journal* detailed the case against an Edward Geraghty and Hugh Keavney who had been accused of assault and trespass at the residence of James McLean of Larkefield near Athlone. James McLean's account claimed he had been threatened and told to quit his residence. He also claimed he was not a Quaker but had been apprenticed to one in Ballymurray.[59] James claimed that he was a Protestant who went to church, and he also went to Mass. His wife Peggy McLean was a Catholic and they went to great lengths to marry in Athlone chapel with a Fr Browne officiating.[60] Edward Geraghty and Hugh Keavney were found guilty and later sentenced to transportation for life.[61] The experiences of former Quakers reflected the strains of life in Co. Roscommon in the early nineteenth century, as a result of pressures on land resources caused by an especially rapid growth in population. The nationwide increase in population between 1821 and 1831 was 14.19 per cent, whereas in Co. Roscommon it was 19.59 per cent.[62] Disturbances grew in frequency during the 1830s and 1840s, many of which are detailed in Anne Coleman's *Riotous Roscommon: social unrest in the 1840s*.[63] It is evident from the cases of John Burne and James McLean that they were considered to be Quakers by the press and members of the wider community many years after quitting Quaker membership. A very small group of Quakers, self-claimed pacifists, who were perceived in a similar manner to the Protestant landed gentry, must have felt isolated, fearful and helpless in their own defence.

By the 1840s the Quaker community in Ballymurray had been reduced to a handful of members. The records of the Moate meeting provide details of the final years of the tiny community. While nothing relating to Ballymurray was recorded in the early 1840s, on 18 October 1844 a report on the Ballymurray meeting was ordered. The report was read at the meeting in Moate on 15 November and a visit to Ballymurray was decided upon. The resulting report was written into the minutes in December 1844 and revealed the decline of the Ballymurray Quaker community. The Friends who wrote the report attended a first-day's service in Ballymurray in November and found that it was held in Rachel Pellet's parlour, which was close to the meeting house. Pellet stated that the room was always ready for the reception of Friends on First days and the usual weekday meetings. The meeting was occasionally attended by another female Friend with her daughter, a young child (most likely one of the Lewis children), and a young woman who was not a member. They were very often prevented from attending, however, by the necessary care she had to give her aged mother who had mobility issues. There was also a male Friend and his child, who lived in Roscommon (William Odlum and his son Robert), but he had not attended for some months prior to December 1845. That was the full extent of the membership of Ballymurray neighbourhood, according to this report.[64]

Friends from Moate were appointed to visit Ballymurray meeting in April 1845, by which point William Odlum of Roscommon town had resigned from the Society of Friends by letter. His son Richard later spent time as a student in the provincial school at Mountmellick, from March 1848 to December 1852, when he left to apprentice with Samuel Fayle of Clonmel, Co. Tipperary.[65] In September 1845 a burial note from Dublin was received for Elizabeth Clarke, who was buried 'by permission' in Ballymurray Quaker burial ground. 'Permission' was required for the use of Quaker burial ground in the case of someone who was not deemed a full or diligent member or attender. Clarke was in her nineties and a widow. She may have been Susanna Alexander, otherwise Clarke, who was disowned in 1818 for 'marrying out'. A burial note for Lawford Burne (who was not in membership) was received in July 1841. The meeting in Ballymurray had 'for some years been seldom held' and Moate meeting sought permission of the provincial meeting in June 1848 for the discontinuance of Ballymurray meeting. The meeting was laid down in 1848, with the premises surrendered to Lord Crofton in 1855, except the burial ground, which was to be preserved and entirely enclosed for the sole use of Quaker burials.[66]

Few Quakers remained in the Ballymurray area after 1848, and they were recorded in Quaker registers for births and deaths. The Lewis family resided in Racecourse, and in 1880 Sarah Lewis, who by then had been widowed, was buried in Ballymurray Quaker burial ground. Several years later a William Siggins was buried there also. His gravestone, which has now fallen, is dated 2 May 1887. William was 81 years old and was possibly the local man who defended the

Quaker meeting house against demolition. His wife Eleonor Wade is buried 2km distant in Kilmeane graveyard where the Crofton family vault is situated.[67] During the six decades of decline for the Ballymurray Quaker community, the members had been tested many times. Sectarian and agrarian tensions, the need to carry arms for defence, a sense of abandonment by both landlords and fellow Quakers, dwindling numbers and an ageing community were some of the challenges that affected Ballymurray. In later years, Quakers of the Ballymurray community remained on their land. Adhering to the limiting Quaker rules restricted their marriage prospects and their ability to prosper within their locality. Some of the remaining Ballymurray Quaker individuals were buried in Ballymurray Quaker burial ground. Their grave memorials do not conform to Quaker practices and are dated after the Ballymurray meeting was discontinued. For those, there was an enduring attachment to Quakerism.

Conclusion

Marrying out usually resulted in disownment from the Society of Friends and in this author's opinion it was a double-edged sword. In the early eighteenth century one of the major difficulties or form of protest for the Quakers was the refusal to pay tithes to the established church. In marrying out, not only were Quaker members marrying a Protestant, but the ceremony was carried out by a priest. These actions would make it difficult to refuse to pay tithes and adhere to Quaker rules. Another reason for not allowing members to marry out was to maintain the family unit and the family associations. We have seen how many of the original Ballymurray Quakers were interrelated. Quakers hired Quakers, worked and networked with Quakers. Diluting the community through marrying out was dissuaded, with disastrous consequences for the Ballymurray Quakers.

The Ballymurray Quaker community survived for 130 years. As this book shows, they were always a small group and in that context their endurance is remarkable. Their relationship with the Croftons of Mote Park and their associations with the linen industry were significant factors in their story from the outset. The establishment of the community occurred in a period marked by a weak economy, poor harvests and the great frost and subsequent famine of 1740–1.

The arrival of the Newport Quakers after the collapse of the Mayo community may have boosted numbers, but it also put more pressure on the struggling Ballymurray families. By the 1740s, the evidence suggests that a close-related community had emerged, but it continued to face problems, internal and external. The difficulties experienced by the Croftons and continuing economic pressures exacerbated the challenges faced by the Ballymurray Quakers. The 1750s marked a decline in the linen industry nationwide and several Ballymurray Quaker weavers left the area for Pennsylvania. It was also notably difficult due to the loss of two community elders and the scandal involving two of the Burne family and their elopement 'to an island on the Shannon'. Marcus Lowther Crofton's finances had been drained on account of the long 'vexatious' lawsuit concerning Mote Park estate, and until his son Edward leased the estate in the 1770s it is probable that little improvement was carried out. The 1786 advertisement seeking Protestant linen workers for a newly proposed linen manufactory in Ballymurray signalled an attempt at regeneration.

As this book demonstrates, the internal dynamics of the Ballymurray Quakers did not always help their cause. The records illustrate the manner in which Quakers lost members, for a whole variety of reasons, but they also suggest a growing willingness to adapt rules in an effort to shore up membership in the face of decline. Despite these efforts, the future of the community was in doubt from the later eighteenth century. As noted in Chapter 3, many former Quakers or their families remained in the locality in the early nineteenth century, but the viability of the Ballymurray meeting was called into question. The visit of the American Quaker Jesse Kersey underlined the scale of the challenge, while the report of 1817 reflected the inability of the community to respond. By the time the meeting was discontinued in 1848, the community had dwindled to just a handful of members.

APPENDIX I

Quaker surnames of Ballymurray and the periods they appear in the Moate Quaker records

Acton	1790s
Alexander	1740s to 1790s
Barton / Burton	1720s to 1820s
Beale	1740s to 1833
Boate	1717 to 1748
Burne	1716 to 1841
Byran	1790s
Church	1720s
Evans	1720s to 1750s
Fairbrother	1750s to 1840s
Gaw / McGaw	1720s to 1800s
Heannan / Kennan	1720s to 1760s
Heaton	1720s to 1730s
Hogg	1730s to 1770s
Hutchins	1720s
Jackson	1718 to 1818
Knott	1833 to 1845
Lewis	1800s to 1848, 1819 to 1880 (Ballymurray Quaker burial ground)
McClung / McClunn	1720s to 1750s
McLean	1720s to 1800
Nevitt	1820s to 1800
Odlum	1834 to 1852
Peck	1720 to 784
Pellet	1785 to 1848
Robinson	1732 to 1830s
Siggins	1716 to 1750, 1799, 1887 ... Kilroy (married Siggins) 1864
Sinklar / St Clare	1717 to 1750s
Sproule (Athlone)	1720s to 1790s
Sutcliff	1720s to 1770s
Taylor	1740s to 1750s
Wigglesworth	1790s to 1830s
Wilson	1719 to 1750

Other names that were recorded (infrequently) by Moate meeting in relation to Ballymurray include Fuller, Gatchell, Hall, Hoare, Mitton, Parvin, Ward, White and Wyly.

Notes

ABBREVIATIONS

a.r.p.	acres, roods, perches
FHLD	Friends Historical Library Dublin, Quaker House, Stocking Lane, Dublin
IMC	Irish Manuscripts Commission
JFHS	*Journal of Friends Historical Society*
MMMM	Minutes of Moate men's monthly meeting
NAI	National Archives of Ireland
NLI	National Library of Ireland
RCL	Roscommon County Library
UL	University of Limerick

INTRODUCTION

1 D.M. Butler, *The Quaker meeting houses of Ireland* (Dublin, 2004), pp 16–17, 136–7.
2 Friends Historical Library Dublin (hereafter, FHLD), https://quakers-in-ireland.ie (accessed 7 June 2022).
3 O.C. Goodbody, *Guide to Irish Quaker records, 1654–1860* (2nd edn, Baltimore, 1999), p. 1.
4 M.J. Wigham, *The Irish Quakers; a short history of the religious Society of Friends in Ireland* (Dublin, 1992), p. 7.
5 *The several acts for the improvement of the hempen and flaxen manufactures in this kingdom* (Dublin, 1719). Copy accessed in Bolton Library collection, UL Library (G.19.10(2)). The copy in Bolton collection includes contemporaneous manuscript notes in the last ten pages (henceforth, *The several acts*).
6 John Bateman, *Great landowners of Great Britain and Ireland* (4th edn, London, 1883), p. 112.
7 Tom Curley, 'Ballymurray as I remember it', *Roscommon Association Yearbook* (1984), pp 86–7.
8 Samuel Lewis, *Topographical dictionary of Ireland* (2 vols, London, 1837), under 'Ballymurry'.
9 Isaac Weld, *Statistical survey of County Roscommon* (Dublin, 1832), pp 460–2.
10 Frizell survey and maps of Mote Park and the Crofton estate, 1777 (NLI, Clonbrock Papers, MS 19672); S. Cooke, 'Survey and map of the estate of the Right Hon'ble Lord Crofton, 1828' (Roscommon County Library).
11 A collection of materials copied from various printed sources relating to the history of Athlone and the surrounding area, 1660–1899 (NLI, Malachy Moran Collection, MS 1543–7), i, p. 519, *Faulkner's Dublin Journal*, 6 Jan. 1784; NLI, Crofton Papers, MS 5904/1.
12 1764 proved will of George Crofton. George left a shilling each to his three sisters but left his property to his three 'Friends', John Burne of Galey, John Burne of Ballymurray and John Nevitt of Ballymurray: H.T. Crofton, *The Crofton memoirs: an account of John Crofton of Ballymurray* (York, 1911), p. 184; *Galway Express*, 14 May 1864.
13 Fitzsimons, 'Quaker records in Ireland', *History Ireland*, 24:5 (Sept./Oct. 2016), p. 43.
14 Maps, surveys and tenant rolls of the Crofton estate, 1704–82 (NLI, Clonbrock Papers, MS 19672; Crofton Papers, MS 8825/5, MS 5904); Cooke, 'Survey', RCL.
15 J.B. Braithwaite, *Memoirs of Joseph John Gurney, with selections from his journals and correspondence*, 1 (1855), pp 326–8; Katherine Fry and R.E. Cresswell (eds), *Memoirs of the life of Elizabeth Fry: extracts*

from her letters and journals, 2 (1847), p. 38; Jesse Kersey, 'The European journal' (www.qhpress.org/quakerpages/qwhp/kej.htm) (accessed 27 June 2022).

16 M.L. Legg (ed.), *The census of Elphin, 1749* (Dublin, 2004); *Elphin census, 1749* (NAI, MS M2464); Irish Court of Chancery bill books, 1627–1884 (NAI).

17 Kenneth Carroll, 'Quakerism in Connacht, 1656–1987', *Journal of the Friends Historical Society*, 54:4 (1979), pp 189–205.

18 Kenneth Carroll, 'Quaker weavers at Newport, Ireland, 1720–1740', *Journal of the Friends Historical Society*, 54:1 (1976), pp 15–27.

19 Isabel Grubb, *Irish Quakers: social conditions in Ireland in the seventeenth and eighteenth centuries as illustrated by early Quaker records* (Cork, 2018).

20 Thomas Wight and John Rutty, *A history of the rise and progress of the people called Quakers in Ireland, from the year 1653–1750* (Dublin, 1751).

21 M.L. Legg (ed.), *Alfred Webb: the autobiography of a Quaker nationalist* (Cork, 1999); Wigham, *The Irish Quakers*, p. 66; Carmel Quinlan, *Genteel revolutionaries: Anna and Thomas Haslam and the Irish women's movement* (Cork, 2002).

22 Glynn Douglas, *Friends and 1798: Quaker witness to non-violence in 18th-century Ireland* (Dublin, 1998). 1793–1810 marks a period of change for Ballymurray Quakers, which replicated the national shift in relation to politics and defence. In 1794 there were twenty-eight meetings in Leinster; by 1820 this number had reduced to nineteen.

23 A.C. Myers, *Immigration of Irish Quakers into Pennsylvania, 1682–1750, with their early history in Ireland* (Philadelphia, 1902); Hiram Wood, *History of the Quakers of Limerick, 1655–1900* (Cork, 2020).

1. THE BEGINNING OF THE BALLYMURRAY QUAKER COMMUNITY, 1716–41

1 Minutes of half-yearly national meeting, 1708–57 (FHLD, MS A.3), 8–11 May 1717.

2 Minutes of half-yearly national meeting, 1708–57, 11 May 1716; Minutes of Leinster province meeting, 1706–60 (FHLD, MS B.2), p. 82, dated 1711;

Minutes of national yearly parliamentary committee, 1698–1729 (FHLD, MS A.56), 21 Dec. 1715, 2 June 1716, 8 Dec. 1727; Grubb, *Irish Quakers: social conditions in Ireland*, p. 12; Wight and Rutty, *A history of Quakers in Ireland*, p. 188.

3 John Bergin, 'The Quaker lobby and its influence on Irish legislation, 1692–1705' *Eighteenth-Century Ireland*, 19 (2004), pp 9–36.

4 Minutes of Moate men's meeting, 1680–1731 (FHLD, MS H.7), 18 June 1718.

5 James Kelly, 'Harvests and hardships: famine and scarcity in Ireland in the late 1720s', *Studia Hibernica*, 26 (1992), pp 65–105; David Dickson, *New foundations: Ireland, 1660–1800* (Dublin, 1987), pp 69–129.

6 Minutes of half-yearly national meeting, 1708–57, 8–11 May 1721; Richard Greaves, *Dublin's merchant Quaker Anthony Sharp and the community of Friends, 1647–1707* (Stanford, 1998), p. 46.

7 Minutes of half-yearly national meeting, 1708–57, 8–11 May 1717; Minutes of Leinster province quarterly meeting, 1706–60, 15 Feb. 1718.

8 Sean Cahill, Gearoid O'Brien and Jimmy Casey, *Lough Ree and its islands* (Athlone, 2006), pp 227–9; Minutes of Leinster province quarterly meeting, 1706–60 (FHLD, MS B.2), 1716–18.

9 Wight and Rutty, *A history of Quakers in Ireland*, p. 215.

10 Minutes of Leinster province quarterly meeting, 1708–57, 5 Nov. 1716.

11 Minutes of half-yearly national meeting, 1708–57, 8–12 Nov. 1716; Survey of Lord Crofton's estate in County Roscommon, 1782, and a rental, 1844–5 (NLI, Crofton Papers, MS 5904); A rent roll of Sir Edward Crofton Baronet's estate in the three counties of Roscommon, Sligo and Limerick together with all the farms he has in his hands this 7 November 1704 (NLI, Crofton Papers, MS 8826).

12 Minutes of half-yearly national meeting, 1708–57, 8–11 Nov. 1717.

13 Minutes of half-yearly national meeting, 1708–57, 8–11 May 1718.

14 NLI, Crofton Papers, MS 8826/2; Membership records of sufferings for

Leinster province meeting, 1719–23 (FHLD, MS B.8), 1719.
15 Membership records of sufferings for Leinster province meeting, 1719–23 (FHLD, MS B.8), 1719.
16 Membership burial register for Edenderry meeting, to 1859 (FHLD, MS E.26).
17 MMMM, 1680–1730, 11 Sept. 1717; Minutes of Leinster province quarterly meeting, 1706–60, marriage certificate dated 5 May 1717.
18 Membership records of sufferings for Leinster province meeting, 1719–23.
19 Goodbody, *Guide to Irish Quaker records* p. 7.
20 Membership records of sufferings for Leinster province meeting, 1719–23.
21 Membership marriage certificates of Leinster province meeting, 1664–1716 (FHLD, MS B.15), pp 162, 184; MMMM, 1680–1731 (FHLD, MS H.7), 15 Dec. 1731; Gershon Boate was married three times: first in 1671 to Mary Fuller, secondly in 1676 to Rachel Ball and thirdly in 1682 to Susanna Bennet (information compiled from Leinster marriage certificates and family lists).
22 Robert Armstrong, 'Boate (de Boote, Boet, Bootius, Botius), Arnold (1606–53) and, Gerard (1604–50)', Dictionary of Irish biography, https://doi.org (accessed 13 Feb. 2022).
23 MMMM, 1680–1731, 16 July 1718.
24 Officially listed on National Monuments Services as RO 06874; on Heritage Maps it is situated in Corgarve, but it was always referred to locally and by the Quakers as Ballymurray Quaker meeting house. On online map-viewer for Roscommon graveyards, the burial ground is situated in Killea.
25 MMMM, 1680–1731, 13 Aug. 1773.
26 *The several acts*.
27 Butler, *The Quaker meeting houses of Ireland*, pp 16–17, 219.
28 Ibid.
29 Minutes of Leinster province quarterly meeting, 1706–60, Mountmellick, 8 Oct. 1720, pp 204–6.
30 MMMM, 1680–1731, 1718–20; Minutes of Leinster province quarterly meeting, 1706–60, Edenderry, 7 Apr. 1722, p. 230.
31 *Faulkner's Dublin Journal*, 6 Jan. 1784 (NLI, Malachy Moran collection, MSS 1543–7); NLI, Crofton Papers, MS 5904/1.

32 MMMM, 1732–55 (FHLD, MS H.8), 1757.
33 MMMM, 1792–1822 (FHLD, MS H.10), 1804.
34 *The several acts*.
35 Luke Hinde, *A collection of the epistles and works of Benjamin Holme* (London, 1754), p. 45; Carroll, 'Quaker weavers at Newport', pp 15–27.
36 D.A. Cronin, *A Galway gentleman in the age of Improvement: Robert French of Monivea, 1716–76* (Dublin, 1995); John Hussey, *The Quakers of Baltyboys, Co. Wicklow, 1678–1800* (Wicklow, 2017).
37 C.I. McGrath, 'Southwell, Sir Thomas (c.1655–1720)', https://doi.org (accessed 26 June 2022); Clare McCormick, 'Whispers on a landscape, the Irish Palatines, 1709–1831' (MA, UL, 2017).
38 *The several acts*.
39 '*Baile Uí Mhuirígh*', https://duchas.ie (accessed 26 June 2022).
40 Crofton, *The Crofton memoirs*; NLI, Crofton Papers, MS 5904/1.
41 Minutes of Leinster province quarterly meeting, 1706–60, Marriage certificate, p. 124.
42 MMMM, 1680–1731, Apr. 1729.
43 Membership testimonials of denial for Moate, 1685–1858 (FHLD, MS H.6), June 1743.
44 MMMM, 1733–55, 1741, 1743, 1744, 1745, 1747.
45 Membership testimonials of denial for Moate, 1685–1858 (FHLD, MS H.6), 7 Sept. 1718.
46 MMMM, 1680–1731, 20 June 1726.
47 Ibid.
48 NAI, Irish Court of Chancery bill book, 1724.
49 MMMM, 1732–55, 1735.
50 MMMM, 1732–55, 15 July 1739.
51 MMMM, 1732–55, Dec. 1731.
52 Membership marriage certificates for Leinster, 1716–75, p. 98.
53 Myers, *Irish Quakers into Pennsylvania*, p. 298.
54 NAI, Irish Court of Chancery bill book, 1727.
55 MMMM, 1680–1731, 21 Dec. 1726.
56 William Gacquin, 'A household account from County Roscommon, 1733–4' in Denis Cronin, Jim Gilligan and Karina Holton (eds), *Fairs and markets of Ireland: studies in local history* (Dublin, 2001), p. 107.

Notes to pages 23 to 32   63

57 MMMM, 1732–55, 15 Feb. 1736.
58 Gacquin, *A household account from county Roscommon, 1733–4*, pp 114–23.
59 MMMM, 1732–55, Mar. 1739.
60 Moate membership mixed records, 1685–1858 (FHLD, MS H.6), p. 48, 7 Sept. 1735.
61 Moate membership mixed records, 1685–1858 (FHLD, MS H.6), p. 64, 5 Sept. 1742.
62 MMMM, 1732–55, 1742.
63 David Dickson, *Artic Ireland: the extraordinary story of the great frost and forgotten famine of 1740–41* (Belfast, 1998), pp 19–21.
64 Carroll, 'Quakerism in Connacht' (1976), pp 189–205.
65 *The several acts*.
66 Kelly, 'Harvests and hardships', p. 71.
67 Minutes of Dublin monthly meeting, 1716–24 (FHLD, MS D.15), 21 Mar. 1720, advice to be given in writing to William Sutcliff from Drogheda on his moving to Connacht.
68 Moate membership mixed records, 1685–1858.
69 Myers, *Irish Quakers into Pennsylvania*, p. 353.
70 MMMM, 1732–55, 1735.
71 MMMM, 1732–55, 1739.

2. BALLYMURRAY QUAKERS AND THEIR LOCALITY, 1741–88

1 Marcus Lowther Crofton, 1747 (NAI, Irish Court of Chancery bill books, 1627–1884); Notice Party – someone who is not a party but who the court decides has a proper interest in the proceedings and should be notified about the hearing so that they can ask the judge's permission to participate, https://niopa.qub.ac.uk (accessed 4 June 2022).
2 Legg (ed.), *The census of Elphin*; Elphin census, 1749 (NAI, MS M2464).
3 Crofton, *The Crofton memoirs*, p. 184.
4 Ibid.
5 *Dublin Journal*, 17, 28 Feb., 31 May 1746.
6 Legg (ed.), *The census of Elphin*, p. xxvii.
7 Ibid.
8 Ibid., p.165.
9 Butler, *The Quaker meeting houses of Ireland*, p. 235; Maria Luddy and Mary O'Dowd, *Marriage in Ireland, 1660–1925* (Cambridge, 2020), p. 36; Wigham, *The Irish Quakers*, p. 61.
10 Goodbody, *Guide to Irish Quaker records*, p. 10.
11 Data compiled from membership marriage certificates of the Leinster province meeting, 1664–1716 (FHLD, MS B.15; 1716–75, MS B.16; 1775–1807, MS B.17; 1812–48, MS B.18).
12 MMMM, 1760–92, Apr. 1760.
13 MMMM, 1740–88, Sept. 1761, July 1772, Jan. 1773.
14 James Kelly, 'The abduction of women of fortune in eighteenth-century Ireland', *Eighteenth-Century Ireland/Iris an Dá Chultúr*, 9 (1994), pp 7–43; Luddy and O'Dowd, *Marriage in Ireland*, pp 181–216.
15 Luddy and O'Dowd, *Marriage in Ireland*, pp 8, 181–216; Testimonies of denial, Moate mixed records, 1685–1858, 11 Mar. 1770, 25 Apr. 1770, 3 Sept. 1773.
16 Testimonies of denial, Moate mixed records, 1685–1858, 11 Mar. 1770, 25 Apr. 1770, 3 Sept. 1773.
17 Moate membership record of births, 1660–1782: 1791 (FHLD, MS H.1, MS H.2).
18 Testimonies of denial, Moate mixed records, 1685–1858, 11 Mar. 1770, 25 Apr. 1770, 3 Sept. 1773.
19 MMMM, 1732–55, Nov. 1749. Sarah Burne and her half-uncle Edward Burne have not been identified from the records, as birth and death records do not appear for either of them.
20 Harman Murtagh, 'Daniel Grose's depictions of the island monasteries of Lough Ree' in Bernadette Cunningham and Harman Murtagh (eds), *Lough Ree: historic lakeland settlement* (Dublin, 2015), pp 110–15. Murtagh references John Cowan's 1773 chart of the Shannon, in which Inchcleraun is named 'Quaker Island' with three houses depicted on it.
21 Cahill, O'Brien and Casey, *Lough Ree and its islands*, pp 227–9; R.S. Harrison, *A biographical dictionary of Irish Quakers* (2nd edn, Dublin, 2008), p. 84.
22 Grubb, *Irish Quakers: social conditions in Ireland*, pp 32–7.
23 Goodbody, *Guide to Irish Quaker records*, p. 38.
24 MMMM, 1732–55, May 1735.
25 MMMM, 1708–1808 (FHLD, MSS A.3, A.4, A.5).

26 MMMM, 1732–55, Nov. 1732; Minutes of National half-yearly meeting, 1708–57, Nov. 1732.
27 MMMM, 1685–1858, 14 June 1772.
28 R.T. Vann and David Eversley, *Friends in life and death: the British and Irish Quakers in the demographic transition, 1650–1900* (Cambridge, 1992), pp 82–165.
29 MMMM, 1732–55, Apr. 1755, Sept. 1756, Jan. 1757.
30 MMMM, 1732–55, Nov. 1715, Apr. 1728.
31 Gerardine Meaney, Mary O'Dowd and Bernadette Whelan, *Reading the Irish woman: studies in cultural encounters and exchange* (Liverpool, 2013), pp 14–53.
32 Tuomo Peltonen, Hugo Gaggiotti and Peter Case (eds), *Origins of organizing* (Cheltenham, 2018), pp 147–68; probably the prequel of 'buy one get one free'!
33 Minutes of Leinster province meeting, 1706–60, p. 212, 1721.
34 MMMM, 1760–92, Nov. 1767 to Nov. 1772.
35 MMMM, 1760–92, Mar. 1765.
36 Leanne Calvert, 'The journal of John Tennent, 1786–90', *Analecta Hibernica*, 43 (2012), pp 69–128; MMMM, 1760–92, Feb. to Sept. 1772.
37 Peltonen, Gaggiotti and Case (eds), *Origins of organizing*, p. 160.
38 Provincial school records for Mountmellick, 1784–1822 (FHLD, MS B.11), 1787–8.
39 Benjamin Bankhurst, *Ulster Presbyterians and the Scottish diaspora, 1750–1764* (London, 2013), pp 4, 33; Christine Kinealy and Gerard Moran (eds), *Irish famines before and after the Great Hunger* (Cork, 2020), p. xiii.
40 MMMM, 1732–55, Jan. 1749.
41 MMMM, 1733–55, 11 Mar. 1750.
42 It is assumed that the scandal of the elopement of Sarah Burne and her half-uncle Edward Burne to Inchcleraun in 1750 fuelled the local renaming of the island as 'Quaker Island'.
43 Bankhurst, *Ulster Presbyterians and the Scottish diaspora, 1750–1764*, pp 4, 33.
44 MMMM, 1732–55, Sept. 1753; Wood, *The Quakers of Limerick*, p. 119.
45 Minutes of Mountmellick men's monthly meeting, 1749–58 (FHLD, MS G.5), Dec. 1749.

46 Dudley Levistone Cooney, *The Methodists in Ireland: a short history* (Dublin, 2004), pp 43–4.
47 MMMM, 1733–55, Mar. 1755.
48 Butler, *Quaker meeting houses of Ireland*, p. 22.
49 MMMM, 1732–55, Jan. 1749, Apr. 1750.
50 Wood, *The Quakers of Limerick*, p. 119.
51 Crofton, *The Crofton memoirs*, pp 114–16.
52 Map and survey 1777 (NLI, MS 19672).
53 Crofton, *The Crofton memoirs*, pp 114–16.
54 Moate membership mixed records, 1685–1858, Apr. 1814.
55 *Faulkner's Dublin Journal*, 6 Jan. 1784 (NLI, Malachy Moran collection, MSS 1543–7).
56 Weld, *Statistical survey of Co. Roscommon*, pp 460–2.
57 *Baile Uí Mhuirígh*, www.duchas.ie, last accessed 20 May 2021.
58 MMMM, 1760–92, June 1790.
59 Membership marriage certificates of Leinster province meeting, 1775–1807 (FHLD, MS B.17), pp 197–8.
60 Murtagh, 'Daniel Grose's depictions', pp 110–15.
61 MMMM, 1760–92, Apr. and May 1786. This John Burne of Rockhill is listed in Richard Harrison's *Dictionary of Irish Quakers*, and John Burne of Rockhill, aged 70, was buried in Ballymurray on 21 Sept. 1826, as recorded in the burial register of Moate meeting.
62 MMMM, 1760–92, Jan.–June 1775.
63 Minutes of national half-yearly meeting, 1757–78 (FHLD, MS A.4), Nov. 1773, May 1774.
64 *Saunders's Newsletter*, 13–15 June 1774; *Freeman's Journal*, 13 June 1774 (NLI, Malachy Moran collection, MSS 1543–7).
65 MMMM, 1760–92, Jan.–June 1775.

3. THE DECLINE OF THE BALLYMURRAY QUAKER COMMUNITY, 1789–1848

1 Crofton, *The Crofton memoirs*, pp 122–4.
2 Minutes of Leinster provincial meeting, 1798–1824, Dec. 1817; MMMM, 1792–1822 (FHLD, MS H.10), Dec. 1817.
3 Betsy Shackleton, *Annals of Ballitore: a compilation of annals of Ballitore by Mary Leadbeater* (Kildare, 2009); Legg (ed.), *Alfred Webb*, pp 24–9.
4 Minutes of National half-yearly meeting, 1778–1808, Apr. 1796; MMMM, 1792–1822, Apr. 1796.

5   MMMM, 1792–1822, 6 Apr. 1796; MMMM, 1792–1822, 4 May 1796.
6   Douglas, *Friends and 1798*, p. 39.
7   MMMM, 1792–1822, June 1797.
8   Douglas, *Friends and 1798*, p. 39.
9   Shackleton, *Annals of Ballitore*; Quinlan, *Genteel revolutionaries*.
10 Minutes of National half-yearly meeting, 1798–1808, Apr. 1798.
11 J.M. Wakefield Richardson, *Six generations of Friends in Ireland, 1655 to 1890* (London, 1894); Legg (ed.), *Alfred Webb*, p. 31.
12 MMMM, 1792–1822, 12 Dec. 1798.
13 MMMM, 1792–1822, 8 Sept. 1802.
14 MMMM, 1792–1822, 6 Apr. 1804.
15 MMMM, 1792–1822, 8 Aug., 19 Sept. 1804.
16 MMMM, 1792–1822, 9 June 1813.
17 Minutes of Leinster provincial meeting, 1798–1824, Dec. 1817; MMMM, 1792–1822, Dec. 1817.
18 MMMM, 1792–1822, Dec. 1817.
19 Ibid.
20 Tithe applotment books, 1823–37 (NAI).
21 Ibid.
22 Moate membership records, births and burials (MS H.6; MS H.19; MS H.18); Lewis' grave memorial at Ballymurray Quaker burial ground.
23 Leinster register of marriages, 1812–48 (FHLD, MS B.18), Aug. 1830.
24 MMMM, 1792–1822, Jan. 1814–Feb. 1820.
25 MMMM, 1792–1822, Nov. 1813.
26 MMMM, 1792–1822, Nov. 1820.
27 MMMM, 1792–1822, April 1821.
28 In the northern section of Tromaun townland, Tervallhall was listed on the 1777 survey of Mote Park and the Crofton estate; the name is now unused whereas the locals call a piece of ground in this vicinity 'the bleach'. This suggests linen production was carried out in this location, and that the name Tervallhall was an anglicization of the Irish word *Tuar*. The ruin of Wade's mill is situated near here and a field name 'the bleach' is known to locals.
29 MMMM, 1792–1822, Dec. 1811, May 1812.
30 Leinster register of marriages, 1812–48, Dec. 1834.
31 MMMM, 1792–1822, Aug. 1818.
32 MMMM, 1792–1822, Dec. 1817.
33 Mixed records of Moate men's monthly meeting, 1660–1782, May 1833.
34 Ibid. The latter part of this quotation is from Isaiah 60:22.
35 Crofton, *The Crofton memoirs*, pp 122–4.
36 Weld, *Statistical survey of the county of Roscommon*, p. 462.
37 Cooke, 'Survey'.
38 The collecting and recording of sufferings were mentioned annually in the minutes of Moate meeting, but individual records for Co. Roscommon Quakers are available for just two periods, 1719–23 and 1788–1832.
39 Kinealy and Moran (eds), *Irish famines*, p. xiii.
40 MMMM, 1792–1822, June 1814, May, July 1815.
41 Moate records of sufferings, 1788–1859, parish cess 1812.
42 Frizell survey and maps of Mote Park, 1777 (NLI, Clonbrock Papers, MS 19672).
43 Cooke, 'Survey'.
44 Charles Rogers, *Memorials of the earl of Stirling and of the house of Alexander* (2 vols, Edinburgh, 1877), ii, pp 46–7.
45 Moate records of sufferings, 1788–1859, 1832.
46 Kersey, 'The European journal'.
47 Fry and Cresswell (eds), *Memoirs of the life of Elizabeth Fry*, 2 (1847), p. 38; Braithwaite, *Memoirs of Joseph John Gurney*, 1 (1855), pp 326–8.
48 Braithwaite, *Memoirs of Joseph John Gurney*, 1 (1855), pp 326–8.
49 *Freeman's Journal*, 26 Mar. 1827. List of nine suspects awaiting trial for John Burne's murder.
50 *Dublin Evening Mail*, 23 Apr. 1827. This article gives details of the auction of all stock of the late John Burne of Rockhill, which listed 700 2-yr-old welters, 100 2-yr-old ewes, 40 cows and heifers, a fine brown mare with foal, 3 fillies, turf, potatoes and manure.
51 *Morning Post*, 27 Sept. 1826. This article gave two accounts of the murder of John Burne.
52 *York Herald*, 30 Sept. 1826; *Morning Advertiser*, 27 Sept. 1826; *Belfast Newsletter*, 26 Sept. 1826; *Freeman's Journal*, 25 Sept. 1826.

53 *Caledonian Mercury*, 28 Sept. 1826.
54 *Dublin Evening Mail*, 29 Sept., 2, 6 Oct. 1826.
55 T.S. Ireland to Major Warburton, 26 Oct. 1826 (NAI, CSO/RP/OR/1826/307).
56 *Mayo Constitution*, 1 Jan. 1829; *Dublin Evening Packet and Correspondent*, 30 Dec. 1828.
57 *Clonmel Herald*, 3 Jan. 1829; *Dublin Evening Packet and Correspondent*, 30 Dec. 1828; *Kilkenny Moderator*, 7 Jan. 1829.
58 *Clonmel Herald*, 3 Jan. 1829; *Dublin Evening Packet and Correspondent*, 30 Dec. 1828; *Kilkenny Moderator*, 7 Jan. 1829.
59 *Freeman's Journal*, 22 June 1831 (NLI, Malachy Moran Collection, MSS 1543–7).
60 Ibid.
61 Ibid.
62 W.E. Vaughan and A.J. Fitzpatrick (eds), *Irish historical statistics: population, 1821–1971* (Dublin, 1979), pp 3–15.
63 Coleman, *Riotous Roscommon*, pp 7–49.
64 Rough copies of Minutes of Moate men's monthly meeting, 1840–56 (FHLD, MS H.21), 18 Dec. 1844.
65 Leinster provincial list of scholars, 1786–1856 (FHLD, MS H.4E).
66 Butler, *The Quaker meeting houses of Ireland*, p. 17.
67 Ibid.

Index

Acton family 59
Alexander family 51, 59
Alexander, Edward 12, 35, 36
Alexander, Elizabeth 31, 37
Alexander, George 31
Alexander, Jane 43, 46, 51
Alexander, John 43, 47, 49, 51
Alexander, Mary (Nevitt) 43
Alexander, Rachell (Nevitt) 43
Alexander, Susanna (aka Clarke) 55
America 18, 24, 34, 35, 52, 58
Athlone, Co. Roscommon 10, 16, 35, 38, 39, 53, 54, 59, 60n11
Athy, Co. Kildare 22
Attiknockan townland 28
Aughrim, Co. Galway 35

Ball, Rachel 62n21
Ballygalda/Stonepark townland 49
Ballymartin Beg townland 49
Barcroft, Deborah 16
Barton / Burton family 59
Barton, Elizabeth (Nevitt) 43
Beale family 59
Beale, Anne née Burne 43, 47
Beale, Jonathan 38
Beale, Samuel 47
Bennet, Susanna 62n21
Boate family 22, 23, 28, 59
Boate, Gerard 14, 17
Boate, Gershon, baby 20
Boate, Gershon, jr 14, 16–18, 20–2, 62n21
Boate, Gershon, sr 14, 17, 21–3
Boate, Hannah 37
Boate, Mary 17
Boate, Rachel 23, 24
Boate, Rebecca see Jackson, Rebecca
Boate, Samuel 23
Bogganfin townland 28, 49
Boggin townland 49
British Army 27
Brown, Peter 51
Browne, Fr 54
Buckingham County, Pennsylvania 22
Burke, Mr 37

Burne family 13, 15, 20, 22, 27, 32, 39, 41, 44, 51, 53, 57, 59
Burne, Abigail née Jackson 20, 22
Burne, Anne 38, 43
Burne, Edward 18, 31, 49, 57, 63n16, 64n42
Burne, George 15, 16, 20, 22
Burne, Godfrey 42
Burne, James 14–16, 20, 22, 26, 29, 34, 44
Burne, James jr 22
Burne, John jr 46
Burne, John of Galey 38, 39, 43, 60n12
Burne, John of Rockhill, Carrownolan 38, 39, 42, 43, 47, 53, 54, 64n61, 65nn49–51
Burne, Joseph 46
Burne, Joseph/James 43
Burne, Judith 20, 31
Burne, Lawford 42, 43, 49, 53, 55
Burne, Mary 38
Burne, Sarah 31, 43, 44, 46, 57, 63n16, 64n42
Butler, David M. 17
Byran family 59

Caledonian Mercury 53
Calvert, Leanne 26, 33
Cantrell, Elizabeth see Gibbs, Elizabeth
Cantrell, John 24
Carlow 16, 17, 41, 45
Carroll, Kenneth L. 12, 19, 21, 24, 25, 27
Catholic 23, 28–30, 37, 54
Church family 20, 59
Church of Ireland 10, 12, 15, 26, 57
Church, Deborah née Wilson 20–2
Church, Richard 20
Churchpark, Athleague 43, 47
Clarke, Elizabeth 55
Clarke, Susanna see Alexander, Susanna 55
Clonbrock, Co. Galway 11; Papers 11; Photographic Collection 11
Clonmel, Co. Tipperary 55
Coillte 8
Coleman, Anne 54
Connacht 7, 12, 13, 18, 19, 22, 25, 52
Cooke survey of Crofton estate (1828) 48, 51
Coolaphubble townland 28
Coolrain, Co. Laois 46

67

Corgarve townland 17, 49, 51, 62n24
Corgorrow/Curgarrow townland 49
Cornamaddy townland 28
Crofton family 8, 10–13, 15–18, 26–8, 36, 38, 40, 41, 48, 56, 57
Crofton Dillon, Augusta 11
Crofton memoirs 12, 27, 36
Crofton Papers 11
Crofton, George 60n12
Crofton, Lord Marcus Lowther, 1st baronet (1797 creation) (d. 1784) 13, 26–8, 36, 41, 58
Crofton, Oliver 26–8
Crofton, Sir Edward, 1st baronet (1661 creation) (1624–75)
Crofton, Sir Edward, 2nd baronet (1661 creation) (c.1662–1729) 14, 15, 17–19, 25
Crofton, Sir Edward, 2nd baronet (1797 creation) (1748–97) 13, 18, 37, 41, 58
Crofton, Sir Edward, 3rd baronet (1661 creation) (1687–1739) 15, 17, 18, 20, 24, 25
Crofton, Sir Edward, 3rd baronet (1797 creation) (1778–1816) 41, 44, 48
Crofton, Sir Edward, 4th baronet (1661 creation) (1713–45) 27
Crofton, Sir Edward, 4th baronet (1797 creation) (1806–69) 48, 51, 55
Curgorrow/Corgarve townland 49
Curry townland 43, 49

Dillon, Luke Gerald 11
Douglas, Glynn 12
Drogheda, Co. Louth 24
Dublin 8, 15, 17, 20, 22–4, 32, 39, 42–4, 47, 55; Trinity College 15

Edenderry 16, 23, 38
Edmundson, William 8
Elphin, diocese 12, 29; census (1749) 20, 26–9, 37
England 24, 48
Evans family 24, 59
Eyrecourt, Co. Galway 38

Fairbrother family 32, 59
Fairbrother, Edward 31, 32, 43, 47, 49
Fairbrother, George of Curgorrow/Corgarve 49, 51
Fairbrother, George of Portrunny 49
Fairbrother, Hannah 30, 32, 43, 47; *see also* Parvin, Hannah
Fairbrother, John 31
Fairbrother, Judith née Burne 31
Fairbrother, Prudence 34

Faulkner's Dublin Journal 18, 37
Fayle, Samuel 55
Featherstone, Lady 31
Fontenoy, Battle of 27
Fox, George 7
Freeman's Journal 54
French, Robert 19
Friends Historical Library, Dublin (FHLD) 10
Friends Historical Society 10
Frizell survey of Mote Park (1777) 37, 51
Frizell, Charles 36
Fry, Elizabeth 52
Fuller family 16, 59
Fuller, Henry 16
Fuller, Jacob 16
Fuller, Jane 16
Fuller, Mary 62n21

Galey Beg townland 28
Galey townland 13, 15, 18, 28, 31, 34, 35, 38, 41, 44, 48–51, 60n12
Galway county 19
Gatchell family 59
Gaw family *see* McGaw family
Gaw, John 29, 50; *see also* McGaw, John
Geraghty, Edward 54
Gibbs, Elizabeth née Cantrell 35
Gibbs, Nicholas 35
Glass family 23
Godin, Mary *see* Godwin, Mary
Godwin, Mary 23
Goff, Elizabeth 30
Goodbody, Olive C. 8, 12
Grubb, Isabel 12
Gurney, Joseph John 52

Hall family 59
Haslam, Anna 12
Haslam, Thomas 12
Heannan family 25, 59; *see also* Heanon family
Heanon family 29; *see also* Heannan family
Heaton family 59
Heaton, Mary 21, 22
Heaton, Mrs (wife of Robert) 32
Heaton, Robert 32
Hoare family 59
Hogg family 59
Hogg, Ann 33
Hogg, Joseph 33
Hogg, William 33
Holme, Benjamin 19
Hutchins family 59

Index

Inchcleraun (Quaker Island) 31, 32, 58, 63n20, 64n42
Ireland, T.S. 53
Irish Linen Board 17–19, 24
Irish Privy Council 17

Jackson family 16, 51, 59
Jackson, Abigail 20
Jackson, John 49, 51
Jackson, Mary 16
Jackson, Rebecca 17
Jackson, Samuel 49
Jessop, Rachel 38; *see also* Pellet, Rachel

Keavney Hugh 54
Kelly, James 24
Kennan family *see* Heannan family
Kersey, Jesse 18, 52, 58
Kilkenny West, Co. Westmeath 21
Killarney, Co. Roscommon 28, 29, 31, 33, 37, 49, 54
Killea 17, 46, 62n24
Killinvoy, Co. Roscommon 16, 49
Kilmeane, Co. Roscommon 8, 16, 49, 51, 56
Kilroy family 59
Kiltoom parish 29
Knockcroghery 23, 51
Knott family 59
Knott, Agnes 16
Knott, Anne née Siggins 34
Knott, Benjamin 34
Knott, Joseph 21

Larkefield, Athlone 54
Leicestershire, England 7
Leinster (Quaker province) 8, 15, 17, 18, 33–5, 39
Lewis family 55, 59
Lewis, Abigail 43, 46
Lewis, George 43, 46
Lewis, Jane née Alexander 46, 51
Lewis, John (d. 1818) 43, 46
Lewis, John (d. 1841) 43, 46, 49, 51
Lewis, Samuel 8
Lewis, Sarah 55
Limerick 19, 35, 36
Little, John 33
Lough Ree 15, 21
Lurgan, Co. Armagh 8

Marystown (Ballymurray) 15, 18
Mayo 12, 25, 57
McClung family 24, 59
McClunn family *see* McClung family

McGaw family 25, 34, 59
McGaw, James 33, 34
McGaw, John 29; *see also* Gaw, John
McGaw, Prudence née Fairbrother 34
McLean family 25, 34, 59
McLean, Elizabeth 34
McLean, James 34, 39
McLean, James of Larkefield 54
McLean, Peggy 54
McLean, Susanna née Nevitt 34, 39
Methodism 35
Mitton family 59
Moate 8, 10, 12, 15, 17, 18, 21–3, 25, 28, 29, 31–6, 38, 39, 41, 42, 44–51, 54, 55, 59
Moate Granoge 48
Monasteroris 16
Moneymore townland 43, 46, 49, 51
Monivea 19
Morning Post 53
Mote Demesne townland 28
Mote Park 8, 10, 11, 13–17, 19, 26–8, 36, 37, 41, 47, 48, 51, 57, 58
Mountmellick 16, 17, 23, 34, 43, 46, 47, 55
Mountmellick provincial school 34, 46, 55
Mountrath, Co. Laois 16, 20
Mullingar, Co. Westmeath 53
Myers, Albert C. 12

N61 7
Neale, Richard 46
Neale, William 46
Nephit, Joseph 22
Nevitt family 22, 43, 46, 51, 59
Nevitt, Elizabeth 21, 31, 37, 43
Nevitt, John 29, 34, 60n12
Nevitt, Joseph *see* Nephit, Joseph
Nevitt, Mary 43
Nevitt, Nathan 25, 31, 34, 35, 39, 42, 43, 51
Nevitt, Rachell 43
Nevitt, Richard 20–2
Nevitt, Susanna 39
Nevitt, William 29
Newfoundland 37
Newport, Co. Mayo 12, 14, 19, 21, 24, 25, 57
Newtown, Co. Roscommon 20, 28, 29, 32, 43, 46

O'Dowd, Mary 26
Odlum family 59
Odlum, Hannah née Fairbrother 30, 47
Odlum, Richard 55
Odlum, Robert 55
Odlum, William 30, 47, 55

Palatine migrants 19
Parvin family 59
Parvin, Hannah 32; *see also* Fairbrother, Hannah
Peck family 25, 59
Peck, John 25
Peck, widow 25
Pellet family 38, 59
Pellet, Mary née Burne 38
Pellet, Rachel née Jessop 38, 43, 46, 54, 55
Pellet, Vincent 38, 43, 46, 47, 49
Pennsylvania 20, 22, 35, 57
Portrunny townland 43, 47, 49
Pratt, John 18, 24
Protestant 11, 13, 18, 19, 27–9, 32, 37, 53, 54, 57, 58

Quaker Island 31, 32, 43, 47, 58, 63n20, 64n42; *see also* Inchcleraun
Queen's County (now Co. Laois) 50

Racecourse, Moneymore 43, 46, 51, 55
Racepark, Moneymore 43
Rathfriland, Co. Down 24
Richhill, Co. Armagh 46
Robinson family 37, 48, 50, 51, 59
Robinson, Anthony 44, 50, 51
Robinson, Anthony, son of Anthony 50
Robinson, Charles 37
Robinson, Elizabeth 31
Robinson, George 37, 50
Robinson, Hannah née Boate 37
Robinson, Jonathan 21, 29, 37
Robinson, Margaret 52
Robinson, Samuel 50
Robinson, Thomas 'Anty' 49
Robinson, Thomas of Galey 31, 45, 49
Robinson, Thomas of Killarney 49
Robinson, Thomas of Moate 49
Robinson, Trench T. 49
Robinson, William 49, 51
Rockhill, Carrownolan 38, 39, 42, 43, 47, 53, 64n61, 65n50
Rockites 53, 54
Roscommon county 8, 10, 14–20, 24, 25, 27, 31, 35, 42, 47, 49, 50, 53–5
Roscommon County Library (RCL) 51
Roscommon parish 29, 49
Roscommon town 7, 16, 53
Ross, Andrew 23
Russell, George 48
Russell, John of Moate 45, 46
Russell, Margaret née Wyly 48
Rutty, John 12, 15

Scarnegirah 15
Shannon river 31, 37, 58
Shragh *see* Srah townland
Siggins family 15, 22, 59
Siggins, Anne 34
Siggins, George 49
Siggins, Margaret 34
Siggins, Thomas 14–16, 26, 35
Siggins, William 49, 55
Sinklar family 20, 22, 59
Sinklar, Mary née Jackson 16
Sinklar, Robert 16, 21, 22
Sligo 14, 15, 20
Southwell, Edward 18
Southwell, Thomas 19
Sproule family 27, 38, 39, 59
Sproule sister 28
Sproule, Joseph 38
Sproule, Sarah 38, 39
Sproule, William 35, 38
Sproule, William jr 38
Srah townland 49, 51
St Clare family 59; *see also* Sinklar
Sutcliff family 25, 59
Sutcliff widow 25
Sutcliff, William 25
Synge, Edward 12, 26, 27

Taylor family 59
Tennant, John 33
Thomastown 48
Tournai, Belgium 27
Turmane probably Tromaun (nr Mote Park) 47

Wade, Eleonor 56
Walby, John 33
Walpole, Abigail née Jackson 20, 22; *see also* Burne, Abigail
Walpole, William 20, 22
Warburton, Major 53
Ward family 59
Waterford 17
Waterstown, Co. Westmeath 16
Webb, Alfred 12
Weld, Isaac 10, 18, 37, 38, 48
Wesley, John 35
White family 59
White, Agnes née Knott 16
White, John 16
Wicklow 17, 18
Wigglesworth family 59
Wigglesworth, Anthony 49
Wigglesworth, Joseph 43, 47, 49

Index

Wigglesworth, Robert 44–6
Wigglesworth, Sarah née Burne 44, 46
Wigglesworth, William 43
Wigham, Maurice J. 12
Wight, Thomas 12, 15
Wilson family 22, 59

Wilson widow 23
Wilson, Deborah 20–2
Wilson, Henry 16, 20–2
Wilson, Mary née Heaton 21, 22
Wood, Hiram 12
Wyly family 59
Wyly, Margaret *see* Russell, Margaret